W9-CMB-567

How Can We Still Speak Responsibly of God?

How Can We
Responsibly

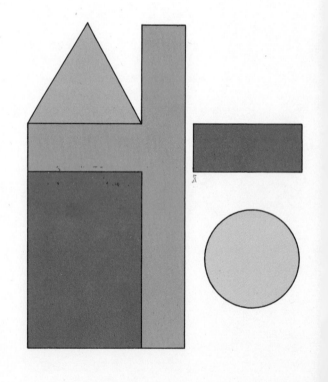

Still Speak of God?

BY Fritz Buri

 Fortress Press *PHILADELPHIA*

The essay, "How Can We Still Speak Responsibly of God?" has been translated by Charley D. Hardwick from *Wie können wir heute noch verantwortlich von Gott reden?* by Fritz Buri (Tübingen: J. C. B. Mohr, 1967).

Preface

The first part of this book was written in late summer of 1966 in preparation for my stay as guest-professor at Drew University, Madison, New Jersey, during the academic year 1966-67. Different parts of this material comprise the substance of lectures delivered during that time, especially in the second semester, at the following institutions: Union Theological Seminary and St. John's University (both of New York), Princeton Theological Seminary, Presbyterian Seminary (Pittsburgh), Wesleyan Theological Seminary (Washington), Yale Divinity School, McCormick Seminary (Chicago), Tufts University (Boston), Andover Newton Theological Seminary, Syracuse University, Ohio Methodist Seminary (Delaware, (Ohio), Southern Methodist University (Dallas), and Temple University (Philadelphia).

The responses I received in the discussions of these lectures indicated that with this theme and my treatment of it I had come upon what is central in contemporary theological discussion in America. After a time devoted mostly to the questions of christology, soteriology, ecclesiology, eschatology, and the hermeneutical problem, the problem of the doctrine of God has again become the center of theological debate, mainly because of the death of God theology. In this connection I also became acquainted with influences not hitherto so familiar to me, such as the positions of Whitehead and Hartshorne, linguistic philosophy, and *Principles of Christian Theology*[1] set forth by John Macquarrie. Although these positions were not considered in the preparation of this material, the insights gained from them do need further consideration and will be the object of a special publication on the theological situation in America. I was surprised to learn, in my contacts with the current theological situation in America, that Barth's influence was never so great in this country, and that even Reinhold Niebuhr and Paul Tillich belong increasingly to the past, as is the case to a higher degree with Emil Brunner. In contrast with other representatives of so-called Neo-Orthodoxy, the thought of H. Richard Niebuhr, whose influence I encountered in quite differ-. ent theologians, proves to be the most formative power in this generation in America. The suggestion that I take Niebuhr's thought as my topic for a colloquium at Yale was made not merely because of a local interest among graduate students at Yale but because of the intrinsic importance of his thought.

Therefore I took into account his early book, *The Meaning of Revelation,* which seems to me to have played a basic role in the education of theological students in this country. There is probably no better means of access to the fundamentals of the theological debate in America. The result of my encounter with his theology is to be found in an appendix to this book. I also used the Niebuhr review in a discussion with a group of colleagues and graduate students in the Department of Religion at the University of Pennsylvania in Philadelphia.

Manifold contacts with contemporary American theology in personal encounter and reading also gave me the occasion to rethink my own position, and to differentiate it more carefully in view of the distinction between the relative subjectivity and objectivity of mental judgments and the all-encompassing subject-object

---

[1] New York: Scribner's, 1966.

schema of our thinking-consciousness. On the basis of this clarification, the meaning of revelation and discourse about God can be approached and formulated in such a way that the interests of the different streams in current American theology can be taken into account without resorting to shortcuts. I believe that such shortcuts are characteristic of the Whiteheadian metaphysicians, as well as of the linguistic and "death of God" anti-metaphysicians. On this basis I set forth in my public lectures at Drew a "thinking faith" which is at the same time a "Christian faith."[2]

During this time I was pleased to receive an invitation from the Harvard Divinity School to deliver the Dudleian Lecture. Following the rule of this institution the lecture for 1967 dealt with the theme of natural religion. Thus I was able on this occasion to use these newly formulated insights in the lecture entitled "The Reality of Faith," which is also reproduced in this book. Discussions which I had at this time with representatives of Zen Buddhism in Philadelphia and with a "Roman Catholic Hindu" at Harvard convinced me that this kind of Christian natural theology can serve as an appropriate basis for a universal human theological thinking in which different heritages can be suitably evaluated for our time. I may mention that I used a part of this second paper at the Divinity School of the University of Chicago, to which I returned once again at the end of my journey through so many centers of American theology.

In view of their common theme and interest as well as in respect to the time in which they were delivered and discussed, the three parts represent a unity. I am grateful to Fortress Press for publishing the lectures in this form. It is my hope that a broader readership will join the hearers of these papers in gaining a better insight into the whole range of the issues at stake and into the perspective which I bring to it.

---

[2] These lectures have been translated by Harold H. Oliver and published under the title, *Thinking Faith* (Philadelphia: Fortress, 1968).

The publication may also be taken as a token of thankfulness for the hospitality and the stimulating response which I received at the above-mentioned places. It is my conviction that further contact between American and European theology can be most fruitful for our common future.

I would like to express my special thanks to Drew University for the opportunity to deliver these papers around the country and for making our stay on its campus such a pleasant experience for my wife and myself.

Finally, I must say that this harvest of my stay in this country would not have been possible without the selfless help of my friends, Dr. Harold H. Oliver of Boston University and Mr. Charley Hardwick of Yale. The former translated the Dudleian Lecture and the latter, the first essay. This book may be considered a result of our *commercium amicitiae* which dates from the time when they studied with me in Basel.

Fritz Buri

Drew University
Madison, New Jersey
April 1967

Contents

How Can We Still Speak Responsibly of God?

To his curiously titled book, *God's Being Is in Becoming (Gottes Sein ist im Werden)*, Eberhard Jüngel—Gerhard Ebeling's successor in Zürich—has given the suggestive subtitle: "Responsible Discourse about the Being of God According to Karl Barth."[1] "Responsible discourse" not only about the Being of God but about God himself, about everything pertaining to God—that would be an excellent definition of the nature and task of theology. Theology is not simply discourse about God, but responsible discourse. This definition of theology contains within itself a criterion for legitimate theology. All discourse about God is not, as such, legitimate theology. But responsible discourse about God—that is legitimate theology.

Now the question immediately arises: responsible before whom and in what way?

To this, Christian theology answers: before God, and, indeed, before the God who has revealed himself decisively in Jesus Christ. Christian theology arises out of this revelation, is indebted to it for its origin, and must again and again reflect on this, its origin, not just for historical reasons but because of the claim which this revelation makes. The salvation revealed in Christ

---

[1] Tübingen, 1965.

applies to the whole world. Christian theology is responsible for this universal claim of revelation. This is the claim it must advocate in the world.

With that, however, something else is already claimed. Christian theology is not only responsible to the revelation of God in Christ but is also responsible *vis-à-vis* the world because of the universality of this revelation. It is responsible for enabling this revelation to be heard and understood by the world. It is to this end that revelation is entrusted to theology, and it must take pains to be understood by the world. Theology is not this revelation; it is rather itself a part of the world—of the world in which it lives. From the standpoint of this, its world, it must raise the question of the meaning that revelation has for its present. It must so speak of revelation that it is revelation today. Thus, theology is mutually responsible to revelation and to the world situation at any given time. It must speak of God in the language of its world.

Without the message of the revelation of God in Christ, there would be no Christian theology. However, theology would not fulfill its task if it did not concern itself with making this revelation intelligible from the standpoint of its time and for the sake of its time.

This twofold responsibility—for the traditional revelation and for the present-day world in which the revelation should be understood—involves a great tension for the nature and task of Christian theology, which can even lead to its breaking apart. Because of the responsibility for the revelation of God entrusted to it, theology can concentrate so exclusively on this revelation that it runs the danger of losing sight of the world to which it must mediate the revelation, with the result that the world does not know what to make of such a theology. Instead of insisting on the purity of doctrine in the face of a deaf world and maneuvering itself into the situation of a voice crying in the wilderness, this

theology should consider the fact that it itself becomes aware of revelation only in the form of a theology of a certain time and that it understands revelation only from the point of view of its own time. So long as its being conditioned by time is not taken into account, the doctrine of the incarnation of the Word is not really taken seriously.

But now theology is also threatened by a danger from the other side. For when it engages the world completely and wants to take its own worldliness with full seriousness, theology may come to take the time in which it finds itself as the criterion of revelation. That is, it might assimilate revelation to the world in such a way that revelation is dissolved in the world and the world becomes revelation. Such a worldly theology must not be judged without reservation as unchristian. On the contrary, it could represent a bold manifestation of the final aim of the Christian revelatory message according to which the lordship of Christ should flow into the kingdom of God, since God will be all in all (I Cor. 15:28). However, it is a question whether the anticipation of this final aim of biblical eschatology is not here purchased at the price of surrendering the reality of Christ's activity in the world proclaimed in Christian revelation. Christ could be so humanized that in him we would no longer have to do with God and his kingdom but only with man and his world. In a world made absolute there is, in fact, no longer any place for the Christian God. Christ would be replaced by man—by a superman, for whom God can only be dead.

Even though both orientations—the orientation to God and the orientation to the world—are mutually demanded in theology, it is already clear from this brief look at the two possibilities that they can also assume opposing, mutually-exclusive forms. It is not merely a question here of a theoretical hypothesis. Both of these extreme forms of interpreting responsibility theologically are present on the contemporary scene with well-defined proposals. Indeed, our theological situation today is essentially defined by this opposition between responsibility before God and responsibility before the world.

To be sure, concerning the first type, which is characterized by a primary—if not exclusive—orientation of its responsibility toward revelation, one can no longer say that it predominates in the contemporary situation in the way that it did for many years. The theology of revelation of Karl Barth and his school, which is in question here, obviously finds its influence declining. It must be satisfied with contributing rearguard actions that incorporate partially altered positions of its opponents. It meets us today, for example, in Eberhard Jüngel's presentation of the basic structure of Barth's doctrine of God, which was mentioned at the beginning.

Today the real polar opposite of the Barthian theology is no longer so much Bultmann and hermeneutical theology—although this theology is still the major scandal to the orthodox communities. The best-defined opposite to a positivism of revelation consists much more in a theology which wants to take with radical seriousness the secularization of the contemporary world and is convinced that one can speak of God only in the language of this world, that is to say, in a nonreligious way. In its most extreme forms this theology has made a slogan of Nietzsche's phrase that God is dead. Representatives of this "theology of the death of God" are, in America, above all William Hamilton[2] and Thomas J. J. Altizer,[3] and prior to them Gabriel Vahanian[4] and, in Germany, Dorothee Sölle.[5] Recently the English Bishop of Woolwich,

---

[2] William Hamilton, *The New Essence of Christianity* (New York: Association, 1961). Cf. also his article in *Playboy* (August 1966), "The Death of God."

[3] Thomas J. J. Altizer and William Hamilton, *Radical Theology and the Death of God* (New York: Bobbs Merrill, 1966); Thomas J. J. Altizer, *The Gospel of Christian Atheism* (Philadelphia: Westminster, 1966).

[4] Gabriel Vahanian, *The Death of God: The Culture of Our Post-Christian Era* (New York: George Braziller, 1961).

[5] Dorothee Sölle, *Christ the Representative: an Essay in Theology After the 'Death of God,'* trans. David Lewis (Philadelphia: Fortress, 1967).

John A. T. Robinson,[6] has also taken up this slogan. But Paul Van Buren[7] refuses it, although from the point of view of linguistic analysis he emphasizes the necessity of a secular theology just as Harvey Cox[8] does from the point of view of sociology.

Although these theologians are descended principally from Bultmann, Gogarten, and Tillich—and, of course, to a certain extent, from Karl Barth—they are no less critical of existentialism in theology than they are of the theology of the Word. Thus, they reject even that theology which stresses the biblical kerygma, the revelation attested in Scripture, and the intelligibility of revelation in the contemporary world. This is so as much today on the part of the secularistic and atheistic theologians as it was formerly by Barth and is still by his followers. In the contemporary discussion, therefore, existentialism truly plays the role of scapegoat for both the Word of God theology and the death of God theology. While the former sees in the personalism of existentialism a betrayal of revelation to the world, the latter judges it as a flight from the world into inwardness.

In order to know what responsible discourse about God can mean today, it will be useful to look somewhat more closely at the above-mentioned two or three basic types, each of which is concerned with responsibility in its own way while denying genuine responsibility in the others.

I. Opposing Types of Responsibility in Contemporary Theology

We begin with the essence of Barth's doctrine of God, which Jüngel has analyzed—or as he says, paraphrased—sagaciously and clearly. Barth is naturally aware of the difficulties which, because

---

[6] John A. T. Robinson, *The New Reformation* (Philadelphia: Westminster, 1965).

[7] Paul M. Van Buren, *The Secular Meaning of the Gospel* (New York: Macmillan, 1963).

[8] Harvey Cox, *The Secular City* (New York: Macmillan, 1965).

of modern man's understanding of the world, history, and himself, face any discourse about revelation and God. But he takes an approach different from other contemporary theologians. Brunner, Althaus, and Tillich—and today, in their own way, even Bultmann and Gogarten—seek a point of contact in the human sphere, an original revelation, a correspondence, or a pre-understanding in order to make the meaning of revelation intelligible and to allow the Word of God to enter the world. Instead of adopting this procedure, Barth strikes out from the other end. He begins not with man and his natural possibilities but with God's Word, which is at the same time God's act in that it has become flesh in Jesus Christ. It has become flesh in order to fulfill the divine decree of salvation to which creation already belongs, which rules history, and which at the end of history will make itself visible to all eyes. For Barth this presupposition of the reality of the divine revelatory action grounds all responsible discourse about God. Theology must think on the basis of this presupposition. Furthermore, it follows from this presupposition that the revelation in Christ has occurred in history and that it can be known in its objectivity through faith, which consists precisely in the acceptance of this presupposition. Faith does not understand revelation in terms of human possibilities of knowledge, nor does it understand the history of God in terms of our concepts of history; rather just the contrary, the latter must be understood in terms of the former, knowledge of revelation and history in terms of the proclaimed and believed salvation. Even the possibility of faith is grounded in the reality of God. Outside the faith caused by God there is no basis for the reality of God, unless in God himself. So Barth replaces any and every kind of natural theology with the doctrine of the Trinity. To the way in which God objectifies himself as the triune One, corresponds the objective manifestation of his decree of salvation in the world, a decree which is structured by his intra-trinitarian nature.

Jüngel correctly points out that in Barth the doctrine of the Trinity has "exactly the same function" as the program of demythologizing in the theology of Bultmann.[9] Just as the necessity for Bultmann to demythologize grows out of responsibility for the historicity of revelation, so Barth grounds this historicity in its correspondence to the intra-trinitarian self-objectification of God. While existentialist interpretation corresponds to demythologizing in Bultmann, Barth understands revelation as "God's self-interpretation."[10] It is obvious that in terms of this concept of revelation, existentialist interpretation can only be judged a betrayal of revelation. According to Jüngel, God's being is in his becoming, insofar as this being consists in the self-interpretation of the trinitarian God. And faith corresponds to this self-interpretation insofar as it does not seek to go behind it but begins with it.

In contrast to Helmut Gollwitzer's emphasis on "God's being-in-himself" in opposition to Bultmann, Jüngel[11] correctly sees that a true polar opposition to Bultmann's existentialism and also to its permutation in Herbert Braun's use of the God-concept as a designation for a "relatedness between men" is reached only in this intra-trinitarian grounding of revelation.[12]

At the same time, however, the problem with this supposedly "responsible discourse about the being of God in Karl Barth" also becomes visible in Jüngel's presentation. How can it still be possible to speak of man's responsibility for his discourse about God when "God as the subject of his being" is "also the subject of his being known and of his becoming known"?[13] If the "yes" of faith

---

[9] Jüngel, *op. cit.*, p. 33.

[10] *Ibid.*, p. 27.

[11] *Ibid.*, p. 101.

[12] *Ibid.*, p. 111, note 146.

[13] *Ibid.*, p. 53. In the *Seinsdenken* of the later Heidegger and in its partial theological use by Heinrich Ott, there is a similar collapse of subject and object in the act of knowledge. Just as in Barth one is not able to tell the extent to which man still knows and believes when, indeed, God is also the subject of His being known and believed, so Heidegger also sees in the expres-

to the "yes" which God says to himself is really caused by God, then man can no longer be held responsible for the sin of unbelief. But then, if sin is that which is not desired by God, how can it have any reality at all? Has God, then, undergone death in his Son because of his own sin? Jüngel does not hesitate to speak in a theopaschitic sense of a "nonbeing of God," of a "powerlessness" and of a "death of God"—a state of affairs which, to be sure, is removed again at once through the resurrection of the Son of God.[14]

What an irresponsible theological outrage arises out of such discourse about God! But neither Barth nor Jüngel seem to be familiar with a responsibility which would shrink from such consequences. Responsibility is exhausted for Barth in that he draws out the consequences of the idea of the Trinity which says "yes" to itself, and for Jüngel by a "paraphrase" of this Barthian doctrine of God. Significantly, after the subtitle the expression, "responsibility," does not occur again in Jüngel's whole treatise. There is responsibility here only in terms of a doctrine of God. And it con-

sion, "thinking of being," both a *genitivus objectivus* and a *genitivus subjectivus.* For this reason, in Ott's book on Heidegger, *Denken und Sein, der Weg Martin Heideggers und der Weg der Theologie* (Zollikon-Zürich: Evangelischer Verlag, 1959), the Heideggerian *Seinsdenken* appears to him well suited to serve as an ontological basis for the Barthian concept of revelation. But that concept of revelation does not become any clearer through this ontology. Instead, its ambiguity is only underlined, as I showed in my essay, "The Problem of Nonobjectifying Thinking and Speaking in Contemporary Theology," given at Drew University in 1964 ("Das Problem des ungegenständlichen Denkens und Redens in der heutigen Theologie," *Zeitschrift für Theologie und Kirche,* 61, 1964, pp. 353-71).

A similar confluence of knowledge and the event of being also occurs in Jürgen Moltmann's *The Theology of Hope,* trans. James W. Leitch (New York: Harper, 1967). Here the truth of proclamation is grounded in the *Sendungsbewusstsein* and this, in turn, as a substitute for the Blochian utopian event, is presented as an *Exponent* of the eschatological event of salvation. (Cf. my essays, "Zur gegenwärtigen Diskussion über das Problem Hoffnung," *Theologische Zeitschrift Basel,* 1966, pp. 196-211, and "Ernst Blochs Prinzip Hoffnung und die Hoffnung im Selbstverständnis des christlichen Glaubens," *Reformatio,* 1966, pp. 211-25).

[14] Jüngel, *op. cit.,* pp. 4, 99 f., 119.

sists in pushing all responsibility off onto God—except for that of the theologian who is responsible for paraphrasing this doctrine and who expects that in the paraphrase God's self-interpretation will take place. And, indeed, this self-interpretation is expected as a "linguistic event." How could it be different when Fuchs and Ebeling are so close at hand![15]

To be sure, as he himself correctly suspects, Jüngel speaks in a language which will be unintelligible to the "poor, average consumer of theology." But what is to be done, then, when the only thing we get is a paraphrase of the doctrine of God's self-interpretation with a "subtilty" which includes the greatest possible problems![16]

One could not imagine a greater antithesis to this theology of revelation than the theology of those who today speak of the necessity of a worldly or even atheistic discourse about God.

Theology which derives from linguistic analysis attacks theological problems by considering their questions and answers in terms of the ordinary daily usage of language and its commonsense logic. In this way it uncovers the inappropriateness of ways of setting problems and the untenability of supposed solutions. Here a very rationalistic, empiricistic, and partially even positivistic spirit rules. In it can still be seen the origin of this analysis of language stemming from the Viennese circle of Moritz Schlick and others. And it seems to correspond very well to the Anglo-Saxon mentality. Metaphysics is here given short shrift, not for theological but for logical reasons. From the philosophical side, existentialism is also sharply denied as a "retreat to commitment"[17] because of scientific and theoretical considerations such as can be found in Carnap and Karl Popper. In his "discourse about God in the language of the world," Paul Van Buren appeals to authorities

---

[15] *Ibid.,* p. 13, notes 25, 43, and 45.

[16] *Ibid.,* p. 118, note 157.

[17] William W. Bartley, III, *The Retreat to Commitment* (New York: Knopf, 1962).

concerning whom he himself grants that they may be basing their criticism of religion on "language learned in Sunday school."[18] Sociological perspectives also play a significant role. Harvey Cox's study of *The Secular City* is essentially a type of sociology of religion both in its biblical, ecclesiological, and theological sections as well as in those sections devoted to an analysis of contemporary society and its origin. Creation, exodus, and the Sinai covenant are presented under sociological perspectives according to which a tribal culture's cultic faith in God was overcome by the metaphysical idea of God in the culture of the city. In turn, this metaphysical idea of God has proved unsatisfactory for the present-day "technopolis." In a world become religionless after the death of God, such a culture can only await a new conception of God.

In all these approaches one sees the great influence of Dietrich Bonhoeffer's demand for a "nonreligious interpretation of biblical concepts" in an age become religionless. Also influential are his assertions that it is necessary to deal with the problems of life "without the working hypothesis of God" and that one must live *"etsi Deus non daretur,"* as if there were no God.[19]

In this connection one is again and again reminded of Nietzsche's assertion of the "death of God" in the chapter entitled "The Madman" in *The Gay Science.*[20] But one can also go back to Hegel's similar assertions in the *Phenomenology of Mind*[21] or even as far back as 1786, to Jean Paul's frightening vision of "the speech of the dead Christ from on high, that there is no God" in his novel, *Siebenkäs.* In an anticritical, apologetic vein, Etienne

---

[18] Van Buren, *op. cit.,* p. 104.

[19] *Letters and Papers from Prison,* ed. Eberhard Bethge (New York: Macmillan Paperbacks, 3rd rev. ed. 1953), p. 195 ff. *et passim.* Cf. also Gerhard Ebeling, "The Nonreligious Interpretation of Biblical Concepts" in *Word and Faith,* trans. James W. Leitch (Philadelphia: Fortress, 1963) pp. 98-161.

[20] Nietzsche, *The Gay Science,* No. 125.

[21] Cf. Robert Garauday's study of Hegel, *Dieu est mort* (Paris: Press Universitaires de France, 1962).

Borne has written his book, *Dieu n'est pas mort* (1965); and engaging this historical development positively, Gogarten's student, Dorothee Sölle, has contributed her book, *Christ, the Representative*, which she has called "an essay in theology after the 'death of God.' "

Penetrating developments in this movement have been made by the two young Americans, William Hamilton and Thomas J. J. Altizer, who have chosen the slogan, "The Death of God," as the motto for their "radical theology." In *The New Essence of Christianity*, Hamilton showed that he was then still strongly under the influence of both French and Italian existentialism (Camus and Silone) and Barth's criticism of religion. Characteristic is his concern for style and language in theology and literature and his interest in concrete problems of ethics, within which his treatment of the problem of marriage wins a theologically central position. Since then, he appears to have come around completely to Altizer's line, as is shown by the praise which he devotes to his friend in his self-presentation as "Thursday's Child" in the joint volume, *Radical Theology and the Death of God.*

From the beginning, Altizer has denied existentialism as a betrayal of worldliness. Even his teacher, Tillich, is for him, just like Eliade, too sacred and not profane enough. Hamilton had already seen the lordship of Christ in his humiliation, his suffering, and his death and had interpreted this as both an answer to the question of God and a guiding principle for ethics. Altizer now picks this up. On the one hand, he views the death of Christ as the self-negation of God, the death of God, the embodiment of all the destructive, senseless, and chaotic elements in the world. On the other hand, he sees in the affirmation of the death of God and of all the negation and emptiness of the world at one and the same time both its dialectical overcoming in the sense of a *coincidentia oppositorum* and an affirmation of the eternal return of the same, as it has been proclaimed by Nietzsche as the victorious

11

act of the Superman in *Thus Spake Zarathustra.* In "Yes-saying" to suffering and guilt the incarnation of God is fulfilled by his death, and the world becomes the body of Christ, the full incarnation of his sacrificial love. Here occurs the final salvation, the victory of a total epiphany of light, as this is envisioned by biblical eschatology. To be sure, Altizer finds the conceptuality and the world of images for this passionately proclaimed "gospel of Christian atheism" less in the Bible than in a kind of Hegelian kenosis christology and in the cosmic-messianic, visionary-mythological poetry of William Blake (1757-1827), in which Jesus, after God has died in his passion, is incarnated in "the Great Humanity Divine."[22]

It is clear that this atheism is different from the atheism of the natural sciences in whose picture of the world there is neither room nor need for the God-hypothesis. But it is also clear that, unlike a scientific atheism, this one cannot be overcome by a critical self-limitation of the sciences. To be sure, in Altizer's reflections, the epistemological question of the possibility of speaking about God in a world ruled by science and technology does play something of a role. But much more than the question of the existence of God, what is at stake in this passionate proclamation of the death of God is the question of the nature of God, the problem of the unification of the evil in the world with the goodness and perfection of its creator, that is, the problem of theodicy. For this reason, these American atheistic theologians—differently from, say, Dorothee Sölle—do not really address themselves to the cognitive question of the existence of God. This was the question which occupied Martin Heidegger from the beginning as the question of the possibility of an ontology, and it is the question which stands behind his vision of the fate of metaphysics in Western philosophy. While Van Buren brings no proper understanding for this

---

[22] Cf. Altizer's essay, "William Blake and the Role of Myth," in Altizer and Hamilton, *Radical Theology and the Death of God,* pp. 171-91.

problem of metaphysics in his empiricistic, linguistic positivism, Bultmann has recently referred to this side of the question of God in his essay, "The Idea of God and Modern Man."[23] Here he refers to the way in which, for Heidegger, the death of God proves to be a necessary result of the "subjectivity" of modern thought. For such "subjective" thought, the world is exhausted by its being objectified so that there is no place for God who, just like Being and existence, is essentially nonobjectifiable.

Just as Jüngel is able to see in the nonobjectifiability of God only an "innocuous assertion,"[24] so also these American theologians do not take into account this fundamental epistemological question of the objectification of thought. In Jüngel or Barth this nonobservance of the subject-object problem takes its revenge in that it never becomes clear whether it is really God or man who believes. In the later Heidegger there is the same ambiguity in the relation between Being and thought. In the death of God theologians, this epistemological unclarity has the effect that they speak emphatically in a remarkable, metaphysical-mythological way of the death of God as an "event in history" while, despite their contrary assertion, it is really a question of a certain conception of God, in particular the Christian one, which has become impossible for them. A God who can be killed, who once lived and who, after the murder of God, is dead forever or for a certain amount of time, presents a highly mythological state of affairs. Such a state of affairs seems singularly odd in the understanding of faith in the theology of revelation, which, indeed, also wants to be something other than religion, as well as in the enlightened, desacralized, scientific-technological world of atheistic religionlessness. Considered in terms of depth psychology, it looks like a still unresolved complex.

---

[23] Rudolf Bultmann, "The Idea of God and Modern Man" in *World Come of Age,* ed. Ronald Gregor Smith (Philadelphia: Fortress, 1966) pp. 256-73.

[24] Jüngel, *op. cit.,* p. 4, note 13.

However, with this epistemological inconsistency is also connected an ethical dubiety, especially regarding the question of
responsibility. This dubiety is no less great in the secularistic and
atheistic theologians than it is in the Barthian theology of revelation. In the latter, seen from the point of view of God, sin is an
"impossible possibility." In the former, it also can no longer play
a role because God, before whom alone there is sin, just doesn't
exist any more and because in the absolutized relativity of the
world one can speak only of relative but not of unconditioned evil.
One can ask himself which one proves itself more ethically problematic, the understanding of the incarnation in Barth's or in
Altizer's sense. Responsibility can only consist, in the one case, in
man's saying "yes" to the "yes" God has said to man in Christ,
and in the other case, in his equally complete "yes" to the chaos
of a world in which God has died. In both instances, there is no
place left for the question of responsibility for the choice of one
or the other possibility. Whether man says "yes" to the Barthian
God or to the relativity and chaos of the secular world without
God—in either case, the responsibility for the choice is removed
by the death of God, which to be sure is very different in the two
cases. For both types of theology, there is only one irresponsibility,
i.e., not choosing the system. With the choice of the system, however, responsibility is removed from man. The system carries the
responsibility, for it itself exhibits a divine process which is
enacted in its affirmation. The believer is justified. As Altizer says
with Nietzsche, for him who says "yes" to the death of God, "all
things dance."[25]

But what about the responsibility we take upon ourselves—
whether we like it or not—when we speak of God's being or His
nonbeing? Neither the theistic nor the atheistic theologians seem
to have considered this question. But it is from just that point of
view that it first becomes possible to catch sight of responsibility

14   [25] Altizer, *The Gospel of Christian Atheism,* p. 154.

at all. It is not God, or Being, or some world process which speaks in theology but rather, for better or worse, merely a theologian. I am responsible for my theology.

Here an entirely different view of responsibility emerges. We do not confront this at all in the choice between a responsibility before God or before the world; if it does seek to emerge, it immediately disappears by the reference to God or the world. But without this question of the personal responsibility of the theologian for his theology, we cannot escape the dilemma between theism and atheism, between theology of revelation and secularism. Therefore, we must now devote ourselves to this aspect of responsibility.[26]

---

[26] It is not presumption but a desire to supply a reference to literature not usually mentioned in this context, which causes me, before we proceed further with the argument, to mention three of my earlier books which stand strikingly close to the present atheistic theologians and, if not an anticipation, nevertheless present in various respects an illustration of their positions. First, *Gottfried Kellers Glaube, ein Bekenntnis zu seinem Protestantismus* (Bern: Verlag Paul Haupt, 1944). As is well known, Feuerbach, whose lectures on the essence of religion he attended in 1849 in Heidelberg, was of decisive importance for the poet, Gottfried Keller. In the *Grüne Heinrich* he dedicated a memorial to him. Secondly, *Prometheus und Christus: Grösse und Grenzen von Carl Spittelers religiöser Weltanschauung* (Bern: Verlag A. Francke, 1945). Spitteler was once a theologian and later a recipient of the Nobel Prize for literature. His mythological-cosmic *Vers-Epen* are an interesting parallel to the poetry of William Blake, to which Altizer refers. In Spitteler's "automation world" of "constrained constrainer" and of a "sick God," man is called to become the redeemer. Finally, *Kreuz und Ring* (Bern: Verlag Paul Haupt, 1947). Under this pair of symbols, I brought together "the young Luther's theology of the cross and the doctrine of eternal return in Nietzsche's *Zarathustra.*"

But all of that was twenty years ago. If in the following I take a different position, then I should like to say in my defense that one cannot remain stuck in a puberty-theology but must develop beyond such positions. Hopefully this will also happen to today's theologians of the death of God, so that they do not fall into a theological arteriosclerosis which only allows one to paraphrase them like epigones.

II. The Nature
of Personal Responsibility

What commends and attracts many to the theology of the Word of God is that this theology appears to have to do not merely with the world and with man but really with God and his Word. The fate of this theology, however, consists in condemning its devotees to the immaturity of its system in that—as impressively illustrated by Jüngel—"responsible discourse about the being of God" can only consist in the paraphrase of a system of the self-interpretation of God. That theology which has sold itself out to a world come of age is burdened with a no less fateful immaturity. Quite apart from the question of how mature our world actually is, one can fall victim to a world that has absolutized itself in its ostensible maturity. Secularism, which has insinuated itself so widely into contemporary theology, gives frightening witness to this fate.

We stand opposed today to all theological and ideological trusteeships which would only like to have us "say in other words the same thing" as they have said. We also oppose a world which thinks it possible to demonstrate its maturity by declaring the old gods dead. Opposed to these tendencies, we consider a truly mature theology necessary, which means a theology that assumes responsibility for its discourse about God, or, more clearly stated, a theology which gives the theologian occasion to become conscious of his responsibility for his discourse about God and world, and to take this responsibility upon himself with complete decisiveness and unconditionedness. To be mature means to take responsibility upon oneself, to push it off on neither a transcendent world, a past world, an environmental world, nor a world to come. It means, rather, to know oneself responsible for oneself in one's world and precisely in this self-responsibility to have to do immediately with God.

16

Without doubt, theology in our time once became aware of this moment of self-responsibility. It was this awareness which brought the concepts of existence *(Existenz)* and self-understanding into usage and which gave them such wide currency during the last three or four decades. But it was also this theology which brought down upon itself the wrath of the theology of the Word and which has recently been repudiated by the secularistic and atheistic theology. It satisfies neither opponent because it wavers between two alternatives and seeks something impossible. I showed this several years ago concerning Bultmann, and the point was taken up with approval by Bultmann's critics.[27] But Bultmann has never contradicted it. Despite his program of demythologizing, this theology in its concept of the kerygma has retained a mythological remainder which cannot be clarified in its self-understanding of faith.[28] From the *existentiell* confrontation with the kerygma, it tries to speak in a so-called *existential,* that is, nonobjective, way. But that is an illusion, a house of cards, as linguistic analysis has also subsequently demonstrated. In the eyes of the theology of revelation what is at stake just as much as ever is the objectivity of salvation in Christ, and it will have nothing to do with the art of existentialist analysis—for which, to be sure, it has almost no understanding.[29] In its eyes, existentialism

---

[27] E.g., Karl Barth, "Rudolf Bultmann—an Attempt to Understand Him," *Kerygma and Myth,* ed. H. W. Bartsch, trans. R. H. Fuller (London: SPCK, 1962) II, pp. 83 ff.; Helmut Gollwitzer, *The Existence of God in the Confession of Faith,* trans. J. W. Leitch (Philadelphia: Westminster, 1965); John Macquarrie, *The Scope of Demythologizing: Bultmann and His Critics* (New York: Harper Torchbooks, 1964) pp. 129 ff. *et passim;* Schubert M. Ogden, *Christ Without Myth* (New York: Harper, 1961) pp. 98, 105-11 *et passim;* Van A. Harvey, *The Historian and the Believer* (New York: Macmillan, 1966) pp. 145 f., 165-68 *et passim.*

[28] Cf. my "Entmythologisierung oder Entkerygmatisierung der Theologie," *Kergyma und Mythos* (Hamburg-Volksdorf: Herbert Reich Ev. Verlag, 1952) II, pp. 85 ff.; and "Theologie und Philosophie," *Theologische Zeitschrift Basel,* 1952, II.

[29] E.g., Oscar Cullman, *Salvation as History,* trans. Sidney Sowers and John Bowden (New York: Harper, 1967).

means the dissolution of *Heilsgeschichte* in subjectivism, an anthropologizing of theology. But today, the secular theologians want not merely a *Christ Without Myth*[30] but a "Christ without God"—a Christ without God who incarnates himself in the world process. Finally the theologians of the ontological Word would like to go beyond the objectivity of our theological language in that, by appealing to Heidegger's *Seinsdenken,* they seek to let salvation occur in the nonobjectivity of a "linguistic event" in which "a place is cleared" for being. However, "the history of the clearing of being" (*die Lichtungsgeschichte*), of which they speak here, proves itself to be, rather, a history of darkness or a smoke-screen history.[31]

In view of this situation, how should any agreement at all be possible, any responsible discourse about God at all, when each one from the standpoint of his own position thinks it necessary to condemn the others for speaking irresponsibly?

Now: neither the leaders of these theological schools nor their adherents, nor anyone, be he a theologian or not, will dispute that when he speaks, writes, and thereby perhaps also thinks about God, when he prays to God, when he calls to him, listens to him, is struck dumb, falls silent, contends with him, or implores him—such a man will not dispute that it is he who does all that; it is he, and not God, not Being, not the world, not a spirit, not another person, not any "it"; rather, he, unmistakably he himself. I am the subject of my speech, my thought, my silence. From the first awakening of consciousness and so long as I am of clear understanding, I find myself in the relationship of a subject to a world of objects. This consciousness can be clouded, it can be overpowered by a transcendent world, by an environment, or by an underworld. It is difficult to speak with unclear

---

[30] Schubert M. Ogden, *op. cit.*

[31] James M. Robinson, "Heilsgeschichte und Lichtungsgeschichte," *Evangelische Theologie,* XXII, 1962, pp. 113-41.

minds, with men who are filled with God, with those possessed, with prophets and fanatics. Such persons do not even understand themselves very well. One can listen to them, try to make them intelligible, and occasionally we are grateful to them for a sobering word. But precisely where we attempt to become clear about ourselves, we are dependent on each other. We must engage in dialogue with each other in order to find ourselves. And the clearer we become with one another concerning our situation, the more it dawns upon us how very much we are stamped and defined in our ideas, our forms of thought, our decisions, our ways of behaving, in short in our entire being—consciously and, to a much larger extent, unconsciously—by our past and our environment. We are what we have become, and we cannot slip out of our skins. Yet, *we* are still what we are, and it is *we* who continually determine what we are through the way we understand ourselves. "At this point, no one else substitutes for us . . ." At this point, I can be neither replaced nor, as Dorothee Sölle believes, represented.[32] Nothing and no one can diminish my responsibility; for that to happen, I would have to extinguish myself as a responsible person. And yet, if it is not the result of events over which I have no control, this effacement of my personal consciousness would still be an act of my personhood. To be sure, this act would never fully succeed, because personhood belongs to my being in such a way that I already find myself in it when I become conscious and it is also still operative when, theoretically or practically, I place it in question or even when I attempt to deny it.

This responsible personhood is not a question of a psychological state of affairs. To be sure, one can speak about it, research it, and expound it—but only in its appearances, which are something different from what personal being and responsibility are in reality. One cannot grasp its reality, because it withdraws from all objectification. It occurs only in its enactment as I become

---

[32] Dorothee Sölle, *op. cit.*, p. 51 ff.

aware of my responsibility, which at the same time constitutes my personhood. A neutral observation of this act of responsibility is not possible, neither in myself nor in another. I cannot observe myself in my personal being—otherwise I would be split in my personhood. What I think about myself is not myself. What I objectively demonstrate and analyze about myself is not myself. The genuine "I" escapes every objectification. That I am responsible, I experience only to the extent that I take responsibility upon myself. The objects with which I thereby have to do and the objectifications by means of which I fulfill my responsibility are not this responsibility itself; they rather constitute only the outer and inner sphere in which it takes place.

The same is true of the personal being of another. I can prove to no man that, in a specific situation, he is responsible. I can only refer him to the situation, accost him concerning it, ask him whether or not he is aware of his responsibility. I can put my trust in him as a person and I can also be disappointed by him. But he himself must understand himself and manifest himself as a responsible person.

As we have already remarked, what is at stake here is more than a question of the theory of knowledge. To be sure, the subject-object schema, within which we inescapably find ourselves in all our imagining, thinking, knowing, and speaking is a basic epistemological structure. And we perceive our responsible personhood only within this structure. But what we here perceive is something different from an object, something which goes quite beyond the sphere of epistemology. It encompasses and permeates our entire existence. It is not just in thought that I know myself to be responsible and it is not just in certain contexts that I understand myself as a person. Similarly, someone else in his personhood does not present for us merely an epistemological problem and does not desire his responsibility claimed only under certain aspects of his

20   personhood. Personhood and responsibility are in self-fulfillment

and encounter, always something whole, encompassing, total, unconditioned, even if, objectively considered, there are distinctions and degrees in the possibilities of personal becoming and in the assessment of responsibilities—distinctions and degrees which are indispensable not only for the clarification of the situation but also for the fulfillment of personal responsibility and for the realization of responsible personhood.

That this matter is by no means merely of theoretical significance but has an eminently practical importance is proved, finally, by the fact that awareness of responsibility and realization of personhood are always bound up with the experience of dissatisfaction and with the knowledge of guilt. Irresponsibility can no more be established nor objectively proven than can responsibility. To be sure, the objective verification of one's own and his fellow man's possibilities, obligations, and shortcomings is necessary and useful for the recognition of responsibility and the guilt which accompanies it. But, as opposed to shortcomings respecting general insights and norms, guilt in relation to personhood can never be objectively established. Guilt is no more an objective matter than responsibility; rather, like responsibility, it demonstrates its unconditionedness only when one takes it upon himself.

When guilt is recognized and taken upon oneself, amends made as far as possible, and works of atonement performed, then a restoration becomes possible both for personal unity, which is threatened by the consciousness of guilt, and for community, which has been broken and endangered through lack of responsibility. Even though the results of culpable behavior and their removal in acts of atonement also belong to the sphere of the objective, nevertheless, because of their connection with guilt and responsibility, reconciliation and the achievement of atonement reach beyond the objective into the mystery of nonobjectifiable personhood. For personhood, neither guilt nor atonement are calculable and therefore relative; rather, they are always personal and unconditioned. 21

Having attempted from several different sides to make clear the mystery of the nonobjectifiability of our responsible personhood in this way, I must add that it is not just at this point where we come up against the limits of objectifiability. On the contrary, along with this nonobjectifiability of the personal, we experience ourselves encompassed and borne in the entire sphere of the objectifiable by a similar mystery of the nonobjectifiable. Not just in our innermost "I" but also at the widest horizons of our physical and spiritual cosmos, we come up against that mystery which announces itself at the limits of our objective knowledge. It is just as impossible for us to know the being of nature and of spirit as a whole as it is to know the "I" and the "Thou." And, to be sure, this is true regarding not only their existence but also their origin. The horizons recede further and further, not just microscopically but also macroscopically. In addition, at every point vertical to the plane on which our ordinary, ceaseless desire for knowledge moves, the question of the origin and ultimate purpose of an already incomprehensible being can arise. This question, which can never be answered, is: Why is there anything at all rather than nothing? Here in the midst of the richness of the cognitive world of objectivity, a nothingness is revealed, revealed not to that desire for knowledge which stops short and settles for provisional results, but to that which always asks more and seeks further and further. Absolutely no statement can be made concerning this nothingness, because it retreats before every attempt to grasp it objectively. Being-as-a-whole is just as nonobjectifiable as the "I" which wants to know itself and the world. For our objective knowledge—and for us there is no other kind of knowledge, i.e., no knowledge outside the subject-object schema—for our objective knowledge, responsible personhood and Being-as-a-whole present a nothingness, the absolute, unattainable boundary of what can be grasped and stated.

22   Personhood is also included in this nothingness of the non-

objective. Just as the unfathomable abyss of nothingness can loom before us at any point in the objective world, so also it can loom in our personhood—insofar as we desire to grasp personhood conceptually. However, insofar as I enact it, insofar as I take my responsibility upon myself from all the various sides we have looked at, this personhood represents a turning point in our argument. Or better said, it represents, in the literal sense of the word, a "jumping-off point." In the enactment of responsible personhood a leap is made, a leap out of objectivity into nonobjectivity.[33] Personhood in its fulfillment is and remains nonobjectifiable. For conceptualization it is a nothingness; but this nothingness, into which personhood transcends, is not a silent nothingness like that of Being-as-a-whole. Out of this nothingness, personhood becomes aware of the voice[34] which calls it to responsibility and discloses to it space and time, a whole world of objectivity, as the place and the opportunity for the realization of responsibility—or, instead it may not disclose this world to us because it can remain mute and withhold itself from us.

Man is creator neither of himself nor of his world. He does not speak the creative word which constitutes him in a likeness to the Creator, discloses the world to him as the sphere of his responsible existence, and places it at his disposal. He can only hear the voice and take over the *dominium terrae* commissioned to him in Genesis 1:28, which he either assumes or, in *hybris* and folly, forfeits. He is not his own redeemer; rather, he experiences personhood and responsibility—in all the peril, perversion and guilt, atonement and reconciliation connected with them—as a

---

[33] Karl Jaspers calls this "the basic operation of philosophy." Among the many places he speaks about this, see the chapter entitled "The Turnabout" in *Philosophical Faith and Revelation,* trans. E. B. Ashton (New York: Harper & Row, 1967) pp. 76 ff.

[34] For the use which is made in the following of this concept of "voice" in connection with responsibility and personhood, the reader is referred to Martin Buber, *Dialogisches Leben* (Zurich: Gregor Müller Verlag, 1947) esp. pp. 151 ff.

grace, a grace which can also fail to occur. (All of this is described in unique fashion in the biblical myth of paradise in Genesis 2 and 3.) The history of man is also filled with tribulation, and he can neither determine its goal nor dispose over its end. The most that is at his disposal is the ultimate irresponsibility of annihilating his own personhood or that of another, and, assuming that he has not fallen entirely away from the graciousness of Being, he cannot even annihilate personhood without feeling dread and horror. There is the riddle of personified evil which seeks to banish responsibility. Yet it has never triumphed in such a way that it can completely extinguish the voice calling it to responsibility—and, with it, the voice which summons to responsibility: "Adam, where art thou?" and to Cain: "Where is Abel, thy brother?"

This voice, its issuing-forth and the human response to it, is what is at stake in all religions and theologies. Christian theology calls it the Word of God which has become flesh in Christ. As indispensable as such myths and speculations are in order to bring to expression the transcendence-relation of human existence (as this transcendence-relation appears in the unconditionedness of personal responsibility) nevertheless, all such doctrines of revelation are questionable and dangerous because, despite denials to the contrary, they give occasion to the temptation that their words, their theologies, might replace that voice to which alone we are responsible.

The more that theology consists in a paraphrase of theological doctrines, all the more does such a theologizing of the voice necessitate a corresponding demythologization. Nevertheless, through such demythologizing, the misrepresentation of the transcendence-relation of our personhood is not eliminated but only replaced by another form of misrepresentation. When an atheistic system wants to perceive responsibility only in the relativities of a world made absolute, it can rob the voice that calls us to

24

responsibility of its concrete unconditionedness—just as that voice can be made into an idol by the various sacralisms of the religions and by the conceptuality of a theology of revelation. In the Gospels it is said that an expelled demon likes nothing better than to return to the purified house, and that he immediately "goes and brings seven other spirits more evil than himself," so that afterwards it is worse than before (Mt.12:43ff). The representatives of the secular city and of the gospel of an atheistic Christianity should mark these words well.

What is at stake for us is neither a demythologized Christ, nor a Christ without myth, nor a Christ without God. Instead, we seek to validate the responsibility of man in the unconditionedness of his nonobjectifiability as the foundation for our discourse about God. We seek to do this in the world and not merely in theological discourse, but in a theology which does not fall prey to the world: in a theology of responsibility.

III. Theology of Responsibility

That theology of responsibility is neither dogmatism nor secularism is shown in that it neither declares as indispensable, as necessary for salvation, one specific appearance in history (for instance, the biblical kerygma) nor that it is ashamed of the historicity in which it awakened (for instance, "the gospel of Jesus Christ" a "power of God for salvation to every one who has faith"—Rom. 1:16). It sees that it cannot manage without its historicity and that it could not replace this historicity arbitrarily with another. But on the other side, it also does not assert that its historicity should be binding on all. Responsibility recognizes that truth is relative to the forms of its expression. This unconditionedness of personhood in historicity—which is something different from an eternal absoluteness valid for all—is what distinguishes faith from superstition.

In conclusion, and with these presuppositions, at least the main points can be briefly stated concerning what responsible discourse about God can mean today on the basis of the Christian tradition.

First. Christian discourse about God can only be in connection with the revelation of Christ attested in the Bible. For us, however, this revelation consists neither in a mythological speculation about the incarnation of the second person of the trinity, nor merely in the historical appearance of the eschatological prophet Jesus and his ethic. It consists, rather, in the event which occurs when men become aware of their unconditioned responsibility. The structures which result from this event allow us to shape and understand our lives. This being-in-Christ must not be bound necessarily to the appearance of Jesus nor to the historical results which have emanated from him, and it is not limited to this context. But the Christian proclamation can be an occasion for this being-in-Christ, although it can also stand in its way, as the history of Christianity sufficiently documents. For this reason, we assume the freedom to appropriate out of the Christian tradition what corresponds to the essence of faith as unconditioned responsibility in personal community and what can be used as an expression for this being-in-Christ.

Second. About such a Christ we cannot speak "without myth" because the awareness of personhood and the appeal to responsibility are dependent on mythological assertions. Precisely in its objectivity (which, in our time, we can no longer replace or create) myth can serve appropriately as the way to articulate this unconditioned responsibility. For although such responsibility in its fulfillment transcends all objectivity, in this fulfillment it is still dependent on objectivity. Responsibility is not enthusiasm, it is rather the clearest, most alert consciousness, because in it the objectivities of thought become transparent for the nonobjective. The image world of mythology is suitable for making objectivity transparent to the unconditioned. True existentialist interpretation does not mean the elimination of mythology; rather, it leads to its proper use as the language of Transcendence.

But also no "Christ without God"! God is the mythological expression for the unconditionedness of personal responsibility. Without mythological discourse about the voice which calls us to responsibility, we cannot achieve clarity concerning the essence of the unconditionedness of responsibility. It goes without saying that this voice addresses us in our language, arises in our hearts, speaks to us from out of our surroundings; and yet, it is not merely the voice of my heart, my neighbor, my situation. In the objectivity of our inner and outer world there is no unconditionedness, but only demonstrable relativity. To be sure, we must not overlook this relativity of our objective world because it serves for the proper enactment of the unconditionedness of our personhood. But in the midst of these relativities occurs the voice, without the awareness of which we do not achieve personhood. This being-in-Christ is not to be spoken about without God—and that not merely in the sense of a "relation between men" (although that also belongs to it); rather, we must speak of it as the transcendent dimension of our personhood, the voice that calls us to responsibility. Of this act—but only of it—could Jüngel's nice formulation be valid: "God takes a lease on human capacities for knowledge and gives them, in this capacity, the possibility of knowledge of God."[35] But in Jüngel's Barth-paraphrase this statement results in an opaque orthodoxy because, unfortunately, it makes no use of the concept of responsibility. But our claim is just this, that we have to do with God when in our conditionedness we experience ourselves leased out to unconditionedness, that is, taken into its service.

Third. This voice gives us the possibility of experiencing the redeeming and creative reality of personhood as the voice of God. What then should hinder us from speaking here of God, and,

---

[35] Jüngel, *op. cit.*, p. 56.

indeed, of a God who is personal? In any case, not the self-im-portant, breast-beating breed of theologians who glory in their atheism! In a suitable variation of a Pauline phrase, one could say of them that they vie against God, but without understanding (II Cor. 10:12). We hold fast to the *persona Dei loquentis* not in the form of a proof for the existence of God nor by using any kind of *analogia entis.* Then it would again be a question of false objectifications and relativizations, of ideologies and possibly even demonizations. However, we do hold fast to it in the form of an *analogia fidei.* By faith is here meant nothing else but the uncon-ditioned knowledge-of-one's-responsibility as it occurs in enact-ment. By analogy is meant nothing else than the personal forms of discourse and thought necessarily used in this enactment. Re-sponsible personhood is that being in which the *per-sonare* (re-sounding) occurs, the sounding-forth and the penetration of the voice of the unconditioned. The locus of its occurrence is not a mysticism of being, an *unio mystica* where the sounding-forth of the voice is no longer distinct from its being-heard and its over-againstness collapses into my personhood. It occurs, rather, in the inviolable overagainstness of the voice of the "caller" and the hearing of the "one called" in the act of decision and obedience.

In this act of hearing we experience what redemption is in the knowledge of the meaning of our personhood, in the knowl-edge of our shortcomings as persons, and in taking hold of the possibility that our personhood can be redeemed after such fail-ures. All of this we experience as grace in all its meanings—prevenient, cooperative, justifying, and sanctifying (*gratia prae-veniens, cooperans, iustificans, sanctificans*). In such experience we also become aware of what creation and consummation is. Creation: not an epistemologically and scientifically questionable —and also unbiblical—*creatio ex nihilo* at the beginning of time; rather, and in the genuine biblical sense, the experience occurring in one's own historicity of the unconditionedness of a creative beginning which creates order in the midst of chaotic relativities, overcoming those relativities by using them as possibilities for the manifestation of this unconditionedness.[36] Consummation does not mean a mere duplication of the original creation—something which would be burdened with the same scientific and philosophical problems as the doctrine of creation. It means, rather, the awareness that one has never attained completion of himself as a person, the awareness of the fragmentariness and imperfection of every embodiment of responsible being, the knowledge that the new creature still lies hidden in the body of the old Adam. It means that the creature in us and around us groans for the revelation of the Son of God, but it also means the emergence of continually new horizons in the expectation of the second coming of Christ and of our transformation into his glory.

When all these aspects of the biblical-Christian tradition— as well as the many other aspects not mentioned here—are understood as forms of expression for human personhood, why should we not speak of God the Creator, Redeemer, and Consummator in Christ? Why should we not use the attributes, the essence, and the being of this God, and finally even the doctrine of the Trinity

---

[36] In this sense, Kant speaks — e.g., in the *Critique of Practical Reason* — of the positing of a new causal series by a free decision of the will which is aware of its duty to the unconditionedness of the ethical norm. It is significant that, as opposed to Jaspers, neither Heidegger nor Ernst Bloch know what to make of this creative freedom of the ethical man in Kant's sense. Instead, the Kantian tension between appearance and being-in-itself is either overcome by a *Seinsdenken* in which man "has overcome himself as subject, which means that he no longer thinks beings as "objects," or a utopian identity of subject and predicate is posited as the goal of material processes. Concerning Heidegger, cf. Walter Schulz, *Der Gott der neuzeitlichen Metaphysik* (3rd ed.; Pfullingen: Günther Neske, 1957) esp. p. 51. Concerning Bloch, see his own *Philosophische Grundfragen, I: Zur Ontologie des Noch-Nicht-Seins* (Frankfurt/Main: Suhrkamp Verlag, 1961). While Heidegger and Bloch sacrifice responsible personhood to their —extremely different—ontologies (in which there is no room for God and his creation), for Kant and Jaspers these concepts are postulates or ciphers of personhood which knows itself to be unconditionally responsible.

in order to glorify His fullness—even if they remain only approximations and are always inadequate?

Fourth. We are aware that to the orthodox this is all too personalistic, to the existential ontologists too much like philosophy of consciousness, to the secularists and atheists too mythotheological. "Where does any objectivity of salvation remain?" bemoans the one. "What kind of a traditionalistic objectivity is this!" cries the second. And the third wants to verify in a way which here could never apply. We ask ourselves: Does not the personalistic interpretation of Christian mythology lead to delusive ambiguities and misunderstandings?

Granted, in relation to personhood and its Transcendence, one cannot speak of unequivocality and general demonstrability in the sense of a rationalistic positivism.[37] We agree that this rational criterion of correctness in the sense of the positivistic verification of objective-conceptual thought has validity; accordingly it is also used by us. But, as should be clear from the foregoing, we are nevertheless convinced that this scientific criterion of correctness is not universal, and, in particular, is of no use in the sphere of the personal—unless in order to make aware of its nonobjectifiability. Assertions of an objective kind—and there is no other kind—are ambiguous and are not generally demonstrable in their truth when they apply to the nonobjectifiable. And personhood in its responsible relation to Transcendence is in principle nonobjectifiable. One cannot have the truth; he can only be in the truth. In the same sense there is also no having-of-Christ in the truth but only a being-in-Christ. One cannot prove personhood; one can only appeal to it, from person to person, "through faith for faith" (Rom. 1:17).

One can also err in presupposing personhood. The witness of

---

[37] This moment of equivocality is emphasized again and again by Jaspers as characteristic of ciphers for existence, and risking oneself with them is seen as indispensable for faith.

personhood can be misunderstood and explained away. The appeal to personhood can remain unanswered and draw a blank. We can fail ourselves in our personhood and misinterpret symbols of personhood. This risk exists. Grace and success can be guaranteed neither magically nor technically.

With the reality of the personal and its appearances, the same is the case as Lichtenberg said of the Bible: "If an ape looks therein, no prophet will look back." Or, stated somewhat more amiably and at the same time more intelligibly: Should a man confront another who does not know about responsible person-hood or who does not want to know about it (and this possibility exists) or who does not want to hear attestations by other persons or appeals to his personhood, then these realities will not be under-stood as that which they want to be and for this other person should be. There, where the voice has come forth or wants to come forth, he will be present only with a concept of revelation, or a theory of *Heilsgeschichte,* or with history, psychology, and sociol-ogy, but not in his own person. As useful as all such concepts and theories are for the clarification of personhood, they can and may not replace it—otherwise they would overstep the area of their competence and rob us of precisely that which they should clarify for us. In that case, instead of making us open to the voice, they would stand in the way of our hearing it and giving an answer. It is a completely unsatisfactory but typically positivistic substitute for this experience of one's responsibility when, in reference to our relation to Jesus, Paul Van Buren thinks it necessary to speak of "blik," of "infectious" efficacy, and of contagiousness.[38] It is impossible to understand properly what is at stake here with such psychological and sociological ideas which are borrowed from biology.[39]

---

[38] Paul Van Buren, *op. cit.* pp. 5, 97 ff., 100-01, 133, 140 *et passim.*

[39] A similar inadequacy marks the attempt by Carl Heinz Ratschow in *Gott existiert* (Berlin: Verlag Alfred Töpelmann, 1966) to satisfy the concerns of the personal with the help of the Lutheran dogmaticians of the seventeenth

Fifth. In addition to the above, a postitivism of revelation or a linguistic positivism does not really know what prayer is but instead makes a perverted use of it or no use at all. Both cases are equally characteristic. Now and then in Barth, prayer becomes magic in that he allows the finger of God to be moved by the

---

century. With their help he seeks to avoid both an anti-metaphysical existentialism and the contradictions of Gollwitzer's "is-propositions." Ratschow correctly sees that the difficulties in our present discourse about God are connected with that *Bewusstseinsdenken* which became so powerful with Descartes. But precisely when he shows how in Protestant Orthodoxy the *essentia Dei* is understood as *actus purus* and the *existentia Dei* as the actualization of God's essence *("essentia actualis* is just *existentia,"* p. 22) and therein thinks it possible to see a correspondence to the "concept of reality in the Old Testament" (p. 73), he does nothing more than think through the inner necessity of the rise of Descartes' *Bewusstseinsdenken.* With that he, at the same time, shows how impossible it is for us again to go behind Descartes. Ratschow himself notes that the identity of essence and existence presupposed in "pre-Cartesian thought" is not valid "for the presuppositions of our spiritual existence" (p. 23 f.). Rather, this identity would only be possible if God is presupposed as *actus purus* (p. 53). As a consequence, He would be known not just through His effects; rather, this "natural knowledge of God" would itself be enacted "in particular, as a work of God" (p. 56). In order to say, "God exists," that which should be demonstrated, i.e., the identity of God's essence and existence, is here simply presupposed or — because it is indemonstrable — simply asserted. And even this is asserted in a self-contradictory way in that it is man who says that God is the subject of His being known. Ratschow's argument is interesting because it shows that the unclarities we confirmed in Barth and Jüngel and in the Heideggerian *Seinsdenken* were already present in the metaphysics of Protestant Orthodoxy. In view of this state of affairs, and Ratschow to the contrary, the metaphysical categories of that Orthodoxy do not appear to us to be at all the means by which "the contemporary questionability of theological assertions can be properly dealt with" (p. 86). Rather, it appears that a new edition of this Orthodoxy requires, just as the first edition did in its time, the clarification of a thought which is conscious of its finitude and its objectivity. The "turn" which "could be helpful for our situation" cannot consist in "stepping behind Descartes" (p. 87), but must lead through the Cartesian *Bewusstseinsdenken* to an objectivity that is transparent for the nonobjectifiability of God and of man as person. Only in this way can Ratschow's natural metaphysic (as well as biblical mythology and trinitarian speculation about a theology of revelation) become a legitimate form for the articulation of human personhood in its relation to transcendence and thereby also of Christian faith in its historicity.

praying man.[40] For the theologians of the *post mortem Dei,* prayer expressly presents an embarrassment, a "relic" of a level of religion which has been overcome. It is really, and quite consistently, replaced with meditation.[41] Prayer is essentially the actualization of the unconditioned relation of responsible personhood to transcendence. Unconditionedness is the dimension in which the voice can be heard, God appealed to, and an answer given to Him, the dimension in which we know ourselves better understood than we could ever understand ourselves. The praying man has to do with a transcendence which is not silent, but which speaks to him and hears him—therefore not in a mystical silence but in objective discourse. But precisely because it is objective discourse, it can also be misunderstood and perverted. It is a risk without guarantee of success; it is grace just as personhood is grace. Prayer is *the* appearance of responsibility; it is nothing else but unconditioned responsibility in its fulfillment. For this reason, the fulfillment of personhood in unconditionedness means prayer.

Theology of responsibility, then, is ultimately theology of prayer. Responsible discourse about God is a discourse about God which arises in and gives evidence of a discourse with God.[42] The

---

[40] Karl Barth, *Church Dogmatics,* III/3, trans. G. W. Bromiley and R. Ehrlich (Edinburgh: T. & T. Clark, 1961) p. 288.

[41] Cf., e.g., Sölle, *op. cit.* pp. 128-29; Hamilton, *The New Essence of Christianity,* pp. 128 ff.

[42] In his *Habilitations* address, "Theologie als Gebet und als Wissenschaft" (*Theologische Zeitschrift Basel,* 1958, pp. 120-32) Heinrich Ott also takes prayer into account as the "experiential foundation" for theology. In fact, he also discusses it in connection with a responsibility which is, as such, not generally demonstrable. Unfortunately, he does not remain with the employment of prayer as a "foundation" for theology but wants, at the same time, to understand "scientific theology" as prayer. Despite good formulations, he thereby finds himself with difficulties and contradictions both in relation to what is valid as science as well as in relation to the role which should belong to prayer. Nothing else is possible when something the enactment of which is nonobjectifiable instead of being brought into relation is identified in principle with something whose essence consists precisely in objectification.

mark of a good theology is not, as has recently been argued, so much its usefulness for proclamation. If and where we have to do with responsible discourse about God is demonstrated much more in its relation to prayer.

Therefore, at bottom, each individual himself can answer the question whether today it is still possible to speak responsibly of God. He needs only to think about the way he prays. The task of theology, then, is to think through from all its various sides that responsibility which occurs here and to unfold it as a theology of responsibility.[43]

Postscript

When I consider the limited familiarity with American theology that was mine when I undertook the discussion in this essay, I now feel like that legendary horseman who, without knowing it, rode over a frozen lake. Since then, the ice has broken, and I have had the opportunity to learn about the true consistency of these theological waters and to become familiar with their various dimensions, depths, and surfaces—from Jona-

---

Ebeling has correctly emphasized that knowledge of God "stands or falls with the possibility of prayer" (*Word and Faith,* p. 352). But in his understanding of "knowledge of God" as "a linguistic event" (*op. cit.,* p. 351) he neglects the dimension of personal response as it is actualized in prayer. Instead of responsibility he speaks only of "giving an answer" or "existing as answer," which man is empowered to do by the Word. "Being responsible" differs from "giving an answer" in that the former so radically questions the legitimacy of that "empowering" of the Word that this question cannot be resolved by a doctrine of Law and Gospel, because this doctrine is itself placed in question. Like all ontology, the recourse to the "linguistic event" proves to be not a substantiation, but an endangering of responsible discourse about God.

[43] Today I prefer "theology of responsibility" to some terms I formerly used, viz., "theology of existence" and "dogmatics as self-understanding of the Christian faith."

than Edwards' "religious affections" and Horace Bushnell to John Macquarrie's "God talk" and Carl Michalson's posthumous "worldly theology." In another context I hope to render an account of this genuine encounter with American theology.

But out of the wealth of material with which I have worked over the past year I should like to call attention here to two recent and important publications and to take a stand toward them in the light of the position represented in this essay. The two writings whose importance is indispensable for the treatment of our theme—and not merely for the theological situation in America —are John Macquarrie's *Principles of Christian Theology* (New York: Scribner's, 1966) and Schubert M. Ogden's *The Reality of God* (New York: Harper, 1966).

Macquarrie's work is significant in that it represents the first full-blown dogmatics carried through on the basis of a type of Heideggerian existential-ontological thinking. As a systematic achievement it is indeed a significant event in recent American theology. By contrast Ogden's collection of essays and addresses contains only the beginnings of a system. What is significant is that all these essays are directed at our present problem and represent an impressive solution founded on the metaphysics of Alfred North Whitehead and Charles Hartshorn.

Both these theologians agree with me in criticizing traditional natural theology and theology of revelation for the sake of a better "natural theology" which takes form as a philosophical theology and reckons with the secular character of our time without falling prey to secularism. In this respect both emphasize the role of existence (*Existenz*) in their ontology or metaphysics: Macquarrie in that the "letting-be" of being becomes grace for the religious understanding of existence, Ogden in that with Stephen Toulmin he has seen the meaningfulness of being as presupposed in ethical existence. What is important in this regard for both is—in taking love as the essence of being—to possess a   35 guarantee that the desire for meaning (*Sinnverlangen*) on the part of human existence is not in vain but finds its fulfillment in God as the Creator and Lord of the world.

I shall not discuss here how each in his own way comes to this objectivity of a meaning of being-as-a-whole and how each portrays it. Suffice it to say that for each of them the problem of the *analogia entis* becomes a burning issue in that they each understand symbols of faith as assertions concerning a relation of religious thought to an objective reality of God—and not "merely" as the assertion of faithful self-understanding.

This is also the point at which each criticizes Bultmann, whom both otherwise highly esteem. They reproach him for running the risk of stranding self-understanding in subjectivity or for having nowhere developed his idea of the necessity of analogical thought, at which he has sometimes hinted. Ogden is highly critical of Bultmann in another place, viz., in relation to the judgment of Bultmann's concept of kerygma as a mythological remainder. But he is lenient with him when it comes to the problem of analogical thinking, in that he attempts a positive evaluation of what he sees as at least a tendency of Bultmann in that direction. Macquarrie, on the other hand, believes that in this connection he must speak only of a subjectivism in existentialism. For both, however, what is at stake—over against a threatening or an actual subjectivism—is the objectivity of God and his salvation.

But the Achilles' heel of both Macquarrie's existential ontology and Ogden's "new metaphysics" is located precisely here: in their insistence on the objective character of God's reality as something absolutely distinct from human subjectivity. To the extent that they attribute objectivity to God and thus place him over against human subjectivity, they not only find themselves contradicting their own intention of going beyond the subject-object scheme of objective thought, but they also expose themselves to the criticism of a thinking that takes this schema seriously. How can a basically nonobjectifying thinking that has gone beyond the opposition of subject and object still speak of the objectivity of God? In terms of the nonobjectifying thinking intended by Ogden and Macquarrie, discourse about the objectivity of God—even if this is meant in some kind of symbolic sense—can only be judged as a retreat into objectifying thought. Then, as something objective, a false deity stands behind the symbol. The same objection is raised, however, from the side of objective thinking, which is aware of—and acknowledges—its limits.

In contrast to a scientific, positivistic absolutization, that thinking which recognizes that the subject-object schema cannot be transgressed comes nevertheless to a true understanding of symbol. Symbol is then seen as an objective assertion concerning that sphere of reality which is essentially nonobjectifiable but which in its relation to the subject of thinking is indeed brought to expression for self-understanding in the objectivity of symbol. As an alternative, then, to Macquarrie's and Ogden's attempt at a nonobjective discourse about the objectivity of God, we propose an objective discourse about the nonobjectifiability of God. The reality of God consists, as regards the likewise nonobjectifiable self-understanding of existence, in its enactment. But this enactment can be actualized only by means of objective thought.

Bultmann thus has good reason for foregoing an ontology of faith. The analogical thinking that he hinted at cannot be carried through in the form of an ontology or metaphysics but is only manifested in the actualization of faithful existence. The task of theology, however, is to guide the realization of such existence whereby ontological and metaphysical speculations can perform an invaluable service as models of thought. For faith *in actu,* the reality of God is no problem at all. For faith, furthermore, the reality of God does not merely signify a lapse into unbelief or superstition, but is rather a legitimate proving ground for the nonobjectifiability of the actualization of faith and for the adequacy of its objective models and of its indispensable conceptuality, as well as for the historical continuity in which faith finds itself and which it claims to represent.

In this light, then, there is also the possibility of a positive appreciation for the theologies of our two fellow participants in the conversation. Though we are not in a position to acknowledge their theologies as valid assertions concerning the objectivity of the love of God as a guarantee for the meaningfulness of responsible existence, we can nevertheless take their speculative questionability as models of attempted clarifications of faith and as witnesses to specific forms of Christian faith with which it is worthwhile to come into conversation.

But it is precisely at this point that we must call attention not only to the epistemological problems of these theologies but also to their material questionability. When, as with Macquarrie and Ogden, being-as-a-whole is identified with the love of God, then not only does that which is contrary to meaning in the world—evil and disruption—become a problem, but the Christian doctrine of redemption also appears to be superfluous. This universal optimism concerning salvation also stands in contradiction to the dualism of the traditional Christian doctrine of the special saving revelation in Christ and to primitive Christian eschatology. The struggle of these theologians with the problem of sin and theodicy is both exciting and in the end disappointing, because the problem of meaning in existence has not been properly conceived. Not without reason has Ogden's theology already been designated as a "theology without Christ"—in that Christ for him has neither a decisive revelatory quality nor a specific reality of being. Just as Ogden finds everything absorbed into a universal event in a process not finally distinguishable from the world, so Macquarrie would have the biblical event of salvation dissolved into the

38

"letting-be" of being in which he understands so many secrets to be hidden.

In contrast to this Heideggerian or Whiteheadian universalism of salvation, we should like to see in the traditional doctrine of the special revelation in Christ—as the creative principle of the new aeon that manifests itself in being in Christ—the indispensably appropriate form of expression for a self-understanding of authentic existence. We understand revelation in a double sense: (1) as a disclosure of being as "nothingness" (*Nichts*) for conceptual thought in the sense of a *theologia naturalis negativa,* and (2) as the awareness (*Innewerden*) of the special possibility of meaning for responsible existence, which can be spoken of only in symbols of faith seen as objectifications of the nonobjectifiable. This schema of a twofold revelation corresponds to the objectivity of all our thinking and to its limitation through the nonobjectifiability of existence and Transcendence.

Transcendence for existence, however, is the philosophical expression for the reality which we find expressed in the idea of Christ and which we recognize anew as the driving force in his history. Such a reality of Transcendence is precisely what must be made intelligible in this philosophical form—but also in a mythology or speculation interpreted in terms of it—for secular thought. Insofar as it is a question—in any discourse concerning the "death of God"—of a protest against all analogical speculations, proofs for the existence of God, or theodicies undertaken independently of existence, this curious theology of the death of God is without doubt correct. It contradicts itself only in the moment that it absolutizes itself and falls into speculation, as happens especially with Altizer.

Having drawn these critical limits, however, we can still say that a "Christ without God" would be preferable to a "God without Christ." It was not without reason that the ancient Christians were put down as atheists by the heathen. Against this reproach a Christian can only defend himself by saying that he exposes the inadmissible objectifications of both atheism and theism and concentrates his theological undertaking on "annulling knowledge in order to make room for faith"—a faith in which existence in community is understood as grace.

The task of theology is not to prove that God is love but to show how love constitutes the fulfillment of human existence (*Dasein*). The latter is possible without the former as a presupposition but can also lead to a genuine confession of the love of God as something which can never be demonstrated but only elucidated ever anew as a cipher of Transcendence for existence. But what would become of all the philosophical and theological elucidation in the world and all the faithful knowing-oneself-borne by the love of God, if one were not surrounded and borne by the love of the brother? As the Apostle says in I Corinthians 13, "And if I have prophetic powers, and understand all mysteries and all knowledge, and if I have all faith, so as to remove mountains, but have not love, I gain nothing."

I should therefore like my present criticism of these two theologians—who stand very close to me theologically and personally—to be understood not merely in a negative sense but as a sign of our bond "in loving struggle" in which alone truth can occur. "Love never ends."

July 1967

The Reality of Faith

I. The Problem
in Past and Present

The central problem of our subject is already apparent in the formulation of our topic, "The Reality of Faith." Is the genitive construction, "of faith," a subjective or objective genitive? Both are possible grammatically, but materially there is a great difference between them. Understood as an objective genitive, the reality of faith means that toward which faith is directed, that which it believes, that which forms the object or content of faith. If the formulation is understood as a subjective genitive, then faith —quite apart from its content—is conceived in its inner nature, that is, as the enactment of a believing subject. The former stresses the objectivity of faith; the latter, its subjectivity. Both can be realities, though each in a quite different way. Just as they are to be distinguished from each other, so each in its own way is to be distinguished from other realities. Faith has a special object-world, and even in its manifestation it represents a special reality.

With the distinction between such different kinds of realities   41 of faith the problem of their interrelationship is also posed. When distinguished from other objects of knowledge, the objects of faith can never be described apart from the act of faith. The object of faith is primarily the content of faith—even when it is evaluated from perspectives other than that of faith. Thus faith in its enactment is never merely preoccupied with its own subjectivity but, even in its inwardness, with objects—quite apart from the fact that it regularly derives from a world of faith and takes form in a context. Just as an objectivity of faith would be dead without personal appropriation, so a faith without objectivity would be empty and abstract.

This is a way of saying that the objectivity and subjectivity of faith cannot be regarded apart from all other objective and subjective realities of human experience and knowledge. Even if faith should raise the claim of a special reality in this way or another, precisely because of this claim it would not be able to evade the question about reality posed elsewhere, but would have to take it into account.

However much this problem has been newly activated in our time, particularly by Anglo-Saxon logistics and linguistics, it is not really new at all, for it is already to be found in the dogmatic systems of Old Protestant Orthodoxy—in fact, as their epistemological substructure. In their definition of faith these theologians distinguished between a *fides quae*—the faith which is believed—and a *fides qua*—the faith through which or in which belief occurs. The former treats of the objective content of faith, the latter of its subjective enactment.

The object of faith comprises God's revelation as it is deposited in Holy Scripture and as it has been normatively formulated in confessions of faith and constantly reformulated in the proclamation of the church. Because it is based on revelation, this objectivity of faith is supernatural. Its content comprises God and his salvation history, which extends from creation, through

42

the fall and redemption through Christ, down to its consummation beyond and at the end of history.

Old Protestant Orthodoxy, however, evidenced interest not only in these objective components, but also in the subjective side of faith. In addition to the relevant treatments in the prolegomena, it devoted a special section to this question under the perspective of the appropriation of faith through the power of the Holy Spirit. Moreover, as time passed, this treatment of the personal appropriation of salvation assumed even greater proportions. The Holy Spirit, through whom the appropriation occurred, forms the principle connecting both sides of faith. The revelatory testimony of Scripture owes both its origin and its function in the believer to the power of the Holy Spirit.

Its connection with this supernatural manifestation of the Spirit is what distinguishes faith from other human theoretical and practical possibilities which appeal to general revelation and the natural endowments of man. Old Protestant Orthodoxy, following the Roman Catholic tradition, conceded to fallen man a certain measure of knowledge and independent power. It also stressed that these natural capacities are quite insufficient for the attainment of salvation.

This way of regarding the problem, typical of the classical form of the Christian doctrine on this topic, can be traced even in the more recent history of theology. With respect to the Protestant development it has to be said that the situation, through the emergence of historical criticism and the modern positive attitude toward man, was altered so that the subjective side of faith became more strongly stressed and its supernatural objectivity receded increasingly behind the subjectivity of the believer. While in Orthodoxy, faith—as supernaturally effected—was directed toward supernatural salvation, now the message of salvation is understood from the perspective of the religiosity of natural man.

Noteworthy exponents of this neo-Protestant development were Schleiermacher with his God as the "Whence of the feeling of absolute dependence" and—in America—Jonathan Edwards with his interest in the "religious affections." In the further course of the history of theology we may mention Albrecht Ritschl and his school, as well as its American parallels extending down to our time in Boston personalism. Resistance toward this subjectivizing of theology from Karl Barth and the so-called Neo-Orthodoxy is well-known, as is the central role of the whole problem in the discussion centering around Bultmann.

Modern existentialists and linguistic philosophers were not the first to be charged with dissolving the objectivity of the biblical salvation history. Already at the end of the last century A. F. C. Vilmar in Marburg countered a "theology of rhetoric" with his "theology of facts." And even if today the speculations of a Whitehead and the thought about Being of a Heidegger stand at our disposal, it has become incomparably more difficult, due to the reign of secularism, to speak of the "reality of God" or of the "being of God," as is evident from the recent attempts of Schubert Ogden and John Macquarrie. It is even more problematic to us when the myth of the "death of God" is being propagated in the age of demythologizing.

The reference to this "Playboy" theology makes us conscious that we are dealing in our theme not merely with an intricate question of concern only to theologians nor with a matter of interest only to the circles of ecclesiastical piety. Hopefully we are confronted with a problem which arrests the attention of those within and without the church, of Christians and non-Christians, and concerning which theologians and lay Christians have to supply answers—not even to speak of those in the pews who ask whether what the minister says still signifies a reality for our time.

II. Three Criteria
of Scientific Thinking

A first step on the way to dealing with the questions posed would be to clarify for ourselves what we do when—in extending a long and manifold history of the problem—we concern ourselves with the question of the reality of faith. There are three distinct characteristics of any thinking and knowing which raises the claim of scientific clarity and appropriateness, and these are valid for all the realms of discourse manifest in the phenomena so distinguished. In the definitions of faith in Old Protestant Orthodoxy and in the methods of modern logistics and the linguistic philosophers, in the theology of consciousness and in renewed theologies of the Word, in our discussions of all these formulations and in our own attempts to speak of the reality of faith—in all these we are dealing repeatedly with the following three peculiarities of any thinking and knowing which raises the claim of scientific clarity and appropriateness.

In the history of our problem as well as in every extension of it, use is made, *first,* of logical conceptuality. *Fides quae* and *fides qua* as well as the so-called language games, Word of God and salvation history as well as historical research and religious experience, subjectivity and objectivity as well as being and meaning are concepts, that is, words which function by designating univocally an intended state-of-affairs. If these designations have also in the main been taken over from the tradition, their significative function has been given to them. In the course of history, then, they not only experience deviations, but new concepts also join them for designating new manifestations and new relationships. Traditional conceptual systems must not only be constantly tested in those spheres where they are employed, but must even be enlarged and newly defined as the sphere of experience is enlarged and deepened. Every age has to determine on the   45 basis of its own experiences and findings what the traditional concepts signify and how they intend them to be employed hereafter as univocal designations of its experience and knowledge.

It should be noted in this case that over against the concreteness and special character of the world of experience, this conceptuality represents an abstraction, an artificial system of signs. Its advantage over immediate experience consists in the fact that it not only structures experience through the ordering of concepts, but also makes it generally communicable. The expression *fides quae* is quite different from the rich treasury of the objectivity of the salvation-history intended by it, but precisely because it is pale and abstract it provides a univocal designation for what is meant in contrast to what is intended in the *fides qua.* This conceptual language is quite different from common language. As much as it serves its purposes, conceptual language makes common language—as indeed the other realms of experience— into a disposable content of its conceptuality. Conceptual language does not speak as "language speaks"; rather it is employed to bring order into the sense and nonsense of that "which language speaks." Furthermore, those for whom "language speaks" need this "sign language" if they wish to clarify for themselves and others what they actually mean.

Second: without the presupposition of the validity of definite logical principles and their application in thinking and knowing, such things as "deducing, ordering, fixing, putting at one's disposal, taking account of, using, and communicating" are not possible. It is self-evident that even those theologians who in the prolegomena of their dogmatics do not expressly mention the principles of identity, of the forbidden contradiction, of the excluded middle and of cause and effect, actually make use in their presentations and debates of the basic principles of logical thinking. The same is true of those who, for the sake of their appeal to the divinely revealed Word, think they have to declare customary logic invalid and to make use of a special logic of the divine Logos, as, for example, in the doctrine of the Trinity. Even the pretentious attempt to invalidate the axioms of logic is made with the help of those axioms and is thus self-contradictory. There are, of course, different systems of logic and thus there is a history of logical thinking; but whenever logical thinking occurs, those axioms are always present and they always emerge and take effect in the modifications of its history. They are not an invention of thinking, but are simultaneously at hand with it. Conceptual thinking is dependent upon them as upon the experience of a reality which is not generated by them, but is only by their help brought into concepts and logical connections.

While the axioms of logic are unchangeable and in themselves represent a closed unity, this cannot be said—as is evident from what has been pointed out previously—of the conceptual systematization in which thinking orders the reality of experience. On the contrary, these systems of thought are changeable and manifold. The inconstancy and manifoldness of the statements of all knowledge—of those which issue from natural knowledge as well as those which appeal to supernatural revelations of faith— are not accidental phenomena grounded in the individuality of individual thinking or of the believer and his historical situation. Rather, this character of knowledge has a twofold cause unavoidable for all thinking:

In the first place, no thinking is absolute, but always remains the thinking of a finite mind which is never able to comprehend Being in its totality. Thus it exhibits itself as finite even in those absolutizings which contest its limits. Even Hegel's idea of an Absolute World-Mind represents the conception of finite mind, however great. The same is true of statements of faith. Even the believer—and he indeed!—who appeals to divine revelation and the testimony of the Holy Spirit will find it inappropriate to speak in the name of God, but will admit to himself and to others the humanness of his speaking about God. What examples we see of the inhumanity and nonsense that result from assertions to the contrary are enough to give shocking evidence of their inappropriateness.

In the second place, as is acknowledged by this distinction between the spheres of a so-called natural knowledge and a supposedly supernatural faith, the material with which we are concerned in our experience and thinking is so manifold that it cannot be approached in one and the same way, just as it cannot be conceived in the same categories. The theology of revelation makes just such distinctions when it speaks of natural and supernatural revelation, of *fides quae* and *fides qua,* and distinguishes the inspired canon of the biblical revelation from the *testimonium spiritus sancti internum.* Similarly, more recent theology appeals to the distinction between natural and historical sciences, opposes judgments of Being with judgments of value, and dissociates itself from religious experiences of value, from existential statements, and from the mysteries of an existential ontology which is said to be quite different from metaphysics.

Already included here are distinctions which the sciences make in their own spheres, and the great variety of methods of research which they employ. It can be taken today as a criterion of the scientific character of a method, that it rejects any claim to being universal and instead speaks at most of a cosmos of the sciences whose principle consists in the fact that the individual sciences must direct themselves toward the particularities of their own areas of investigation so that each may attain results which are valid only for its area and which are therefore always relative and hence constantly open to future corrections. Thus one speaks today even of an historicality of the sciences.

It is basic to this *third* characteristic of methodical conceptual thinking, the finitude of its subject and the infinitude of its object, that we can speak of the reality of faith only in judgments which are more oriented either toward the object of faith or toward the subjectivity of the believer, and that we are therefore never in a position to make a unified and final statement about the reality of faith. This is richly illustrated from the fragmentary history of this problem to which attention was called initially; it is also characteristic of our present situation.

This state of affairs represents no dilemma for the sciences, for they demonstrate their scientific character precisely by taking full account of it, in that they dispense with the question of the *An-sich* character of reality and content themselves with the verifiability of their statements within the context of their possibilities of knowledge. There are scientists, of course, who do not respect these boundaries with regard to statements of faith, but theology also, from the perspective of its own task, finds itself in a difficult situation insofar as faith in the appropriation of its object assumes an unconditioned position, even though its object is not scientifically verifiable. Thus it is only too clear that theology appears to be a curious science and that faith sees itself more threatened than advanced by science.

III. The All-Encompassing Subject-Object Schema

In order to resolve this dilemma in which we find ourselves when we speak of the reality of faith and thus take into account the conceptual-logical character of this discourse and its methodological consequences, we have to consider another dimension as well, a dimension within which we are already inevitably operating in discourse of this kind. Our consideration of the hitherto neglected situation of all our conceptual-logical, methodical-scientific pronouncements about reality is so constituted that all discourse about reality appears to be jeopardized to an even greater degree than was the case hitherto. But if we do not ignore this state of affairs with which we have henceforth to deal, it becomes a means of access to reality, and especially to the reality of faith. What is at stake here?

Briefly said, it is the fact that with all our objective and/or subjective thinking and speaking about reality which never represents univocally and finally the one or the other but always a mixture of both, we are constantly enclosed in a quite different subject-object relationship which is definite and absolute rather than relative. All thoughts and pronouncements about reality intend an object, that is, are directed toward an object. This is true both of the reality to be thought and expressed, and of this thinking and expressing itself, even when it is directed toward itself. Even this reflexive or—in Kantian terms—transcendental thinking has an object, namely itself, which as the intended object is to be distinguished from intentional thinking and expression by its conceptuality and enactment.

Likewise, this thinking and expression directed toward an object presupposes a subject which enacts the thinking and makes the pronouncements. This subject is something quite different from the intended object-world and from the relation to this object-world. It is *in* this relationship, but it *is not* this relation which it enacts—even though it belongs to its essence. And if it makes itself into its own object— whether reflexively or transcendentally —in this act of viewing itself it is—and constantly remains—the object of its being a subject.

When we think, we always think something if we think at all; and all statements are statements about something, if they are really statements. It is equally certain that it is *I* who think, when I think, and that is *I* who make statements, when I express something. When I awaken to thinking consciousness and enact thinking, this subject which thinks and the object which is thought are already present. For thinking consciousness, subject and object are discrete, but they are not to be separated from one another, since they belong indissolubly together.

All thought and expression occurs in this subject-object schema, and everything which we think—and about which we make statements—also stands in this dichotomy of subject and object, which forms not a split of consciousness but the substructure of its unity. Precisely in the fact that it understands itself in its subject-object dichotomy to be a unity, does this thinking consciousness distinguish itself from a pathological division. There is, of course, a kind of thinking in theology and philosophy in which no account is taken of this essential structure, thus reminding us of the attitudes and utterances of schizophrenics.

It may have become clear in this connection that in the subject and object with which we have to do in this subject-object schema of our thinking-consciousness, there is something dimensionally and principally different from that which is subjective and objective in that knowledge and faith of which we have spoken and which for conceptual, scientific thinking appears at times more subjective, at times more objective. The latter concerns qualities of our judgments which always remain ultimately relative; the former points to the basic structure of our thinking-consciousness in general. The subject-object dichotomy of thinking-consciousness is not the result of an act of thinking; rather, every act of thinking presupposes this schema as the basic structure in which it occurs. This schema is not relative, but absolute. Therefore it cannot be more or less overcome in the course of thought and research—as can the subjectivity of knowledge—but always appears as its fixed boundaries which demand recognition. Even when the greatest possible objectivity is reached, we always operate in the context of this schema; that holds true whether the objectivity is striven for scientifically or simply asserted on the basis of divine revelation.

It is to be conceded in any case that we come to consciousness 51 and clarity about this subject-object schema only with the aid of conceptual-logical thinking, and that such consciousness can itself be made into an object of conceptual-logical thinking—and grasped with a certain measure of clarity—only in this way. It can be falsely psychologized or conversely ontologized or hypostatized. But then the "philosophical ground-operation"—as Jaspers calls it—which signifies its perception is not yet achieved. The unfortunate consequence will be that one is then moving within a pseudo-science or in mythologizing and speculation.

While a psychologizing pseudo-science is to be rejected *a limine,* the case is different with the myths of the religious world and the speculations of philosophy. To become aware of the Encompassing of the subject-object schema has of course as its final consequence the awakening out of the dream-world of myth and the knowledge of speculative thinking as such. When, on the contrary, a scientific criticism, rational and empirical in nature, believes it can dispense with mythology and become freed from speculation, it becomes mythological and speculative itself because of its uncritical trespassing of its own boundaries. This is especially true if it does not acknowledge the content and function of myth and philosophical speculation to be the language of the nonobjectifiable Unconditioned for personal existence in community against the background of the Naught.

Before we turn our attention to this positive side of the subject-object schema as the presupposition within which alone the specified reality of faith can properly be expressed, I should like to be permitted a personal remark. I must admit that in my previous publications—and even in the Prolegomena of my *Dogmatik*—I did not distinguish as sharply as above between a constantly relative objectivity of scientific knowledge and the absolutely comprehensive objectivity of the subject-object schema of thinking-consciousness. This is evident in the fact that I customarily paralleled the latter objectivity with logical conceptuality, methodical appropriateness, and historicality as one of the four characteristics of scientific thinking. It is certainly the case that the subject-object schema of our thinking-consciousness can be clarified only with the aid of logical conceptuality, and that the characteristics of scientific knowledge represent its effect. But in order to express its character as the fundamental structure of thinking-consciousness it is not sufficient simply to mention it first. Such a sequence can lead to a misunderstanding about its significance which in its comprehensive manner is something quite different from the permanently relative judgments of our faculty of knowledge, namely, its presupposition. Just as the dimensional difference which exists between the relative subjectivity and objectivity of all our knowledge and absolute objectivity as the fundamental structure of our thinking-consciousness, is clearly and univocally established, it may now be possible to speak univocally and convincingly of that which was always our concern within this schema, namely that which is not only relatively but unconditionally nonobjectifiable.

IV. The Nonobjectifiable

We ourselves, as those who are conscious that we think in this subject-object schema, are the first "object" which in all its unavoidable objectivizing is more than these objectifications. What we perceive of ourselves, how we experience ourselves, the image we make of ourselves, what we think and say about ourselves—these do not grasp our "I" which in its perception, experience, representation, knowing, and expression, is conscious of itself as the subject of all these acts. Awareness does not occur apart from these acts of consciousness, but the personal existence of which I become aware in them is always more than all that which becomes conceivable in my consciousness. In these terms I can take myself into account more or less subjectively or objectively. But none of the forms in which and through which this happens is this "I" which understands itself in this way. Just as certainly as this "I" only becomes what it is through the way in which it understands itself, it is nevertheless even in its authenticity not objectifiable. Despite whatever may be objectively demonstrated to be conditioned, this observation about the "I" is unconditioned rather than relative.

That which is unconditioned with respect to our personal identity is not demonstrable. If we identify our "I" with objectifications of it, we lose our personal identity in precisely that way. In the "hall of mirrors" of our self-reflections we are constantly in danger of becoming "self-thinkers, self-hangmen," as Nietzsche said. But apart from a pathological split of our self-consciousness we would not be able to extinguish this personal responsibility of our personhood. We are captive within the objectifications of the subject-object schema of our thinking consciousness—but the act of self-understanding is not objectifiable since the "I" which is understood therein is a self. In that act we encounter unconditioned reality which demonstrates its unconditionedness against all attempts to deny it. The reason for this is that even in denial of the self there is still the self which attempts the denial. Once our selfhood has emerged, we can alter it for better or worse, but we cannot lose or annihilate it. Despite all attempts to veil or question selfhood, it persists as that which is veiled or questioned. Despite its demonstrability or lack of it, in the risk of the unconditionedness of its enactment, it wills to come to itself as responsible personhood.

The unconditionedness of responsible personhood, which from an objective point of view may even seem highly questionable, we cannot claim for ourselves alone. We must also concede it to other beings for whom we have to take into account this peculiarity when we wish to do justice to their destiny. Even if it is a fact of our experience that the sphere in which we deal with personhood is limited to human beings, we are nevertheless reluctant to speak here only of man as such, because personhood as we understand it is not an anthropological term; it rather transcends the science of anthropology as well as all possible formulations in psychology and sociology.

In the sciences of man we deal with objectifications within the subject-object schema of our thinking-consciousness, rather than with the personhood manifest and intended in these objectifications. We encounter this unconditioned responsible personhood in the self of the other only where we appeal to this reality in the other or are met by his appeal to our personhood. It must accordingly be said that we understand ourselves in our personhood not apart from other personhood, but only in personal community with it. This is true even though the slogan that we understand ourselves only from the perspective of the Thou, represents in our eyes a theory that does not correspond to personal becoming, because no theory at all is able to grasp the event-character of this reality.

However much we are dependent upon the analysis of objective manifestations for our understanding of the other person, neither personal community nor personhood can be proven or organized; for, in contrast to all certainties, personhood represents a risk which can fail as well as succeed, and which even in disappointments exhibits itself as a destiny which will attain fulfillment. We are destined for personhood; here is a reality whose unconditioned character is not provable because it is nonobjectifiable.

Personhood is, however, not the only sphere in which we encounter a reality of the kind with which science as such cannot deal because it is restricted to that which is conditioned. Even in the sphere of Being as such, despite its possible personal character, we encounter this reality of the nonobjectifiable, i.e., the nonobjectifiability of Being-in-its-totality. Here the way also leads through our relatively subjective and objective judgments beyond the sphere of the objectifiable. At the fixed boundaries set for our knowledge by the subject-object schema, the way opens out upon the question for which there is no answer, which does not in turn call for another question, namely, that question which is unanswerable for our objective thinking: "Why is there something rather than nothing at all?"

In this final question of conceptual-objective thinking—the question about the why of Being, about Being in respect to its Non-Being—we are not dealing merely with the horizon of everything objectifiable, an horizon which constantly recedes before all our investigation and knowledge. Nor are we dealing simply with the fact that all Being is in its objectifications always only a Being-for-us, that is, seen from our standpoint. Nor is this a concern merely with the relativity and historicality of our knowledge and the impossibility of a total view of Being-as-such. Rather, the quest for Being-in-its-totality has to do with the struggle to grasp the inconceivability of its character as reality. And concerning this it cannot be denied that we may despair of but never doubt the reality that we are destined for personhood, because even in such despair we confirm the reality itself.

The nonobjectifiability which we encounter here is twofold: On the one hand, it consists of the Naught which emerges when we seek to give a cognitive answer to the question we have been discussing, since every answer occurs within the subject-object schema. An answer which is not approached through this schema —and such would *have to be* the case with an answer to that question—is not possible in the objectivity of this schema. Outside this schema we cannot grasp Being—it is the Naught. Outside this schema there is nothing we can grasp. But apparently there is this Naught outside the subject-object schema. This Naught manifests its unconditionedness precisely in the fact that, for our thinking, there is in this schema only the conditioned—with the exception of the unconditioned of personhood.

To see the answer to the question about the why of Being in this unconditioned of personhood, as has happened in all constructions of an "Absolute I" as the "World-Ground," would not only contradict the unconditionedness to which the I is destined, but would also have to be expressed in the subject-object schema and would thus confirm that it is Being-for-us rather than Being-in-itself. Just as the self-absolutization of the "I" is impossible in the subject-object schema, so certainly in the recognition of its boundaries does it encounter Being as the Naught. For thought which is within the subject-object schema, Being which is not simply Being-for-me is identical with the Naught.

But, on the other hand, this is not the sole statement with respect to Being which is possible for thought. Just as certainly as Being is inaccessible to this schema, and every attempt to go beyond it leads further into the Naught of the nonobjectifiability of Being, so the Naught is not the only reality which we confront here. For when we take seriously the fact that we are unconditionally destined for personhood, we encounter in the midst of the Naught and outside of it the nonobjectifiable reality of "being called and destined" for personhood. If this being-destined occurs in the sphere of our personhood and has to be realized in it, then we are dealing not merely with a possibility immanently demonstrable to human existence as such, but with a nonobjectifiable reality of one who destines, which is to be distinguished from the nonobjectifiability of the reality of human personhood.

Against this distinction it is not to be argued that no distinction can be made in the sphere of the nonobjectifiable. For, first, conceptual thinking permits such a distinction with respect to the appearances of the unconditioned in its objectifications, and, further, an identification of the destined with that-which-destines would prevent the enactment of responsible personhood. Given with the awareness of Being destined to unconditionedness is the reality of that which destines in its entire nonobjectifiability; and the relatedness of the responsible "I" to a corresponding "Thou" of another personhood provides here the only appropriate designation for the reality, as an absolute personal power, of that which destines to unconditionedness. It is a personal power which represents the origin of Being and gives us the possibility of fulfilling the meaning of our personal existence.

What we, in our relationship to the co-human Thou, have rejected as an unjustified statement—namely, that we understand ourselves principally from the perspective of the Thou of the other, in that we are understood by him—the same is true without restriction of that Thou by which we know ourselves called to the realization in existence of our personhood. It is that Thou which the language of religion describes as "power" or "powers," which here are called "God" or "gods," and which the Christian faith employs in intercourse with its God and the One, or Trinity. The result of this is that the exclusivity of its claim can be both an expression of human will to power and of the unconditionedness which emerges in faith as the enactment of personhood. Whether the result is superstition or faith cannot be decided objectively but becomes apparent as this relation to transcendence is confirmed—especially in one's attitude toward other phenomena of the religious world.

V. A Program of a Christian Natural Theology

It can be asked whether we have succeeded in this way to that which is usually designated as natural religion, that is, to a possibility of an acknowledgment and exaltation of supernatural powers, a possibility given with human existence as such, for the purpose of realizing the meaning of human existence in the world. Or do we attain thereby to a Christian natural theology in which 58 the *fides quae* is completely absorbed into the *fides qua,* so that the former is understood as the expression of the latter and both are demonstrated and justified to the extent that they correspond to reason in its highest surge upward? The question begs for an answer, and an affirmative answer is neither in the one case nor in the other to be rejected out of hand.

If our fundamental insight into the nonobjectifiability of personhood, its realization in personal community, and the relatedness of both to a transcendence which from the perspective of the Naught as it appears for objectifying thinking can manifest itself as person—if that insight itself represents a radical criticism of all objectifications, organizations, and cultic matters of the religious world—we still must deal in those nonobjectifiabilities with matters that are the real concern of the religions: their faith, their world of gods and demons, their communities and cults. In all objectifications of their myths and magical practices, their revelations, visions, and speculations, they intend the nonobjectifiable, as their opposition to the dissolving criticisms of science shows. The sciences also concern themselves with the nonobjectifiable when they fall victim to superstition by absolutizing their methods, techniques, and world-pictures. Even nihilism has to do with faith and transcendence when it unmasks the idols of religion and science and lets itself be exposed to the Naught; it could be on the way to a genuine faith itself if it did not capitulate to new idols. In any case, nihilism affords an indispensable contribution to faith's purification from all objectifications. Although the deobjectification bound up with the philosophical ground-operation represents a crisis of faith, faith nevertheless is actualized only through this narrow pass, as we have shown. This possibility of a realization of faith is grounded in man's true nature. The realization of faith belongs to the nature of man as a creature destined for unconditioned responsibility.

Therefore: Why not natural religion? If the concept is not misunderstood anthropologically and a demonstrable system derived from it, but is understood in the sense of the criticism of the objectifications of religion in its intercourse with the Nonobjectifiable, then nothing is to be said against it.

Nor is the possibility of a Christian natural theology to be opposed from this stance. Even if the Christian faith in its religious formulations, although not finally because of its theology, is subject as all other religion and theology to the danger of superstitious objectifications and dogmatic absolutizings and, as its history shows sufficiently, has often succumbed to such in ecclesiastical and theological systems, it nevertheless carries within itself material originating in the Christian message which is disposed to placing in question all its objectifications, to indicating the nonobjective in its self-denial and transformation, and to providing the occasion for the realization of the nonobjective in faith. Christian faith in its origin is not eschatological in vain; it is devoted to the final questioning of all inner-worldly possibilities.

In this sense we are able not only to demonstrate that which in the tradition of Christian doctrine corresponds to positions represented by us, but also to establish this Christian natural theology from the perspective of our presuppositions in such a way that it does not succumb to the problematic character of false objectification, but serves as an adequate expression for the reality of faith. What is proposed here implies nothing less than the program of an entire dogmatics, something which cannot here be developed, even in outline.[1] We must settle for a few hints.

First. From what we have said above, it may have become clear that the relative objectivity of scientific knowledge and the radical nonobjectivity of the self-understanding of unconditioned personhood in its relatedness to transcendence as presented in the

---

[1] Permit it to be said in this connection that I have developed this program in my *Dogmatik als Selbstverständnis des Christlichen Glaubens* ("Dogmatics as the Self-understanding of the Christian Faith") Bern: Verlag Paul Haupt, Vol. I, 1956; Vol. II, 1962; Vol. III, in progress.

context of the subject-object schema of thinking-consciousness represents what is dealt with in the prolegomena to Christian dogmatics as *knowledge, faith,* and *revelation.* Faith, when it is understood as unconditioned responsibility that can be enacted only with the help of objective conceptuality, is freed from the difficulties which are usually involved in its relationship to knowledge. This is true despite the fact that in this enactment of its self-understanding faith shows itself to be just as nonobjectifiable as the Transcendence of which it is aware in the consciousness of its unconditionedness.

Second. This Transcendence is that God whose twofold revelation involves a *revelatio generalis sive naturalis* and a *revelatio specialis sive supernaturalis* in the classic Christian doctrine of revelation. We here avoid both the dilemma of an impossible contrast of knowledge and faith, and a relative connection between them, by exposing the revelation of the Naught as what is nonobjectifiable to knowledge in the subject-object schema. This allows us to perceive from the Naught the call of the personal God to responsible personhood.

Third. On this basis there is the possibility of an understanding of Scripture as a witness to faith to be investigated historically. Because of its symbolic form, however, Scripture is to be understood only from a faith-perspective.

Fourth. In this way we attain to an understanding of the divine image in man as his irrevocable call to personhood. Furthermore, the fall into sin is understood as a perversion of this destiny which appears as an unavoidable fate in the fact that we can speak of the nonobjectifiable only in objective ways and, therefore, must first experience personal guilt from within faith. The dimension of "responsibility" distinguishes such faith from mere tragic self-understanding.

Fifth. Related to this is a view of the salvatory work of God in Christ in which we become aware of grace which is not at our

61

disposal and not to be manipulated. This occurs when we partici-pate in the reality of faith despite the sinful character of our inevitable objective discourse about the nonobjectifiable.

Sixth. The doctrine of creation in Christ, if conceived in this fundamental way, is not a cosmological and cosmogonic myth-ology or speculation; rather *creatio ex nihilo* expresses a new be-ginning not traceable back to an objective cause, but occurring in the freedom of our responsible personhood in Christ. For this new beginning of a causal nexus in the self-understanding of uncondi-tioned personhood and its realization, space-time is grace, and history the sphere of the *creatio continua,* i.e., covenantal history.

Seventh. The people of this covenantal history form the Body of Christ, the church, which is present wherever this community occurs—whether in Christian or non-Christian, traditional or new forms.

Eighth. The parousia of Christ, the eschatological reality, is the crisis and significative fulfillment of human culture.

Ninth. Finally, the doctrine of the Trinity as symbol of the fullness of God represents the most suitable expression—at least within the Christian world of ideas—for the fullness of faith's relatedness to transcendence. For the community of those who live in this faith-world, the Trinity of God the Father, Son, and Holy Spirit forms not merely a problem for the history of doctrine but the object of its worshipful praise, in which it knows itself to be united with believers—from everlasting to everlasting.

What is signified in these nine points dare not be taken as objective Christian faith to be appropriated by the believer. This would only bring us back to the schema of the subjective and objective, of the *fides quae and fides qua,* from which prob-lematic we have emerged. In the context of the subject-object schema of our thinking-consciousness and the dialectic of the objectivity and nonobjectivity of statements of our self-under-

standing, we can only indicate certain ways in which the reality of faith can occur and be expressed within the special historicality determined by the Christian tradition. Just as a so-called natural theology is realized within the acknowledgment of this historicality—a character based on the appeal to a universal structure of thinking consciousness—so it cannot be expressed in this context apart from that which in "revealed" theology is intended by "the reality of faith." This reality of faith which is attested only by appealing in each case to the self-understanding to be newly enacted—this reality is not a standpoint, but a way through which men, under the guidance of the Logos, can attain to the truly engaging biblical confession, "Out of his fullness have we all received, grace upon grace."

Appendix

The Reality of Faith in H. Richard Niebuhr's
The Meaning of Revelation

I. NIEBUHR'S POSITION

It seems to me that the question of the reality of faith could be a basic point of view for an evaluation of the late H. Richard Niebuhr's *The Meaning of Revelation*. When he explains in the first chapter "The Point of View" he will follow, he himself becomes chiefly concerned, although in different ways, with the problem of the reality of faith.

First, he acknowledges that for our time historical relativism has become most influential and as inevitable for knowledge as for faith. Historical relativism means

> that the spatio-temporal point of view of an observer enters into his knowledge of reality, so that no universal knowledge of things as they are in themselves is possible, so that all knowledge is conditioned by the standpoint of the knower . . .(7)[1]

He goes on to say that even logic is in this sense historical (9, 12). At the same time he stresses, however, that this "does not imply subjectivism and skepticism"(18).

Relative to this he mentions that empirical science always operates with an "acceptance" of the "independent reality" of the object which it searches out. He calls this acceptance of an independent reality "an act of faith," an "animal faith," a "confidence in the objectivity of experience's core." This same faith

---

[1] All citations from H. Richard Niebuhr, *The Meaning of Revelation,* New York, The Macmillan Company, 1962. (First published in 1941.)

he sees operating in the field of history; though this faith can be justified by its fruits, it is nevertheless a faith (20).

For theology, according to Niebuhr, historical relativism means that it is not only forced but indeed justified in beginning with the standpoint of the historic Christian faith. This is a faith in which

> a reality discloses itself which invites all the trust and devotion of finite, temporal men. Such a theology of revelation is objectively relativistic, proceeding with confidence in the independent reality of what is seen, though recognizing that its assertions about that reality are meaningful only to those who look upon it from the same standpoint (22).

From this combination of God's revelation as an independent reality with, in man's historical situation, faith as its complement, he calls attention to Luther's comment that "faith and God hold close together" (23). He sees "the great empirical theology of the nineteenth century" beginning with Schleiermacher and inclusive of Ritschl as a development of this point of view (23 ff.). But what he rejects in that theology is the fact that it became a "faithology" or a 'religionology" which

> turned attention away from God to religious feelings and tended to make the religious consciousness the object of confidence (28).

In opposition to this religiosity, which defended the superiority of the Christian religion only as an important element in human spiritual and cultural life, he refers to "the preaching of the early Christian Church," which was

> primarily a simple recital of the great events connected with the historical appearance of Jesus Christ and a confession of what had happened to the community of disciples (43).

The purpose of the second chapter of Niebuhr's work is to show how it is possible to deal with the reality of this faith in a time of historical relativism. This can be done without losing the reality of God's revelation in a mere confidence in man's religious ideas about God. This chapter attempts to regain a theology of revelation and is significantly entitled, "The Story of Our Life" (43). Here Niebuhr remembers anew the parallelism between theology and science when he says:

> A Jesus of history apart from the particular history in which he appears is as unknown and as unknowable as any sense-object apart from the sense-qualities in which it appears to us (52).

In this parallelism there is still, however, a dualism which is to be found in the method of understanding which we must use to evaluate such an event as Jesus.

Thus, at this point Niebuhr makes his basic distinction between an "outer history of things" and "an inner history of selves":

> Events may be regarded from the outside by a non-participating observer; then they belong to the history of things. They may be apprehended from within, as items in the destiny of persons and communities; then they belong to a lifetime and must be interpreted in a context of persons with their resolutions and devotions (63).

He describes the two different methods, contrasting them as impersonal and personal, pure reason and practical reason, descriptive and normative, suppressing value-judgment as much as possible and marked by commitment, involving quantitive and qualitive time. But then he says that

> one cannot point to historic events in the lives of selves as though they were visible to any external point of view (73)

and that we are confined to a "double and partial knowledge" (84). Nevertheless, he rejects any knowledge of "double reality" (84).

To avoid the conclusion of a double reality—which would mean the rejection of one or the other as nonreality, as an illusion —he refers for a third time to a parallelism between faith and natural experience, but now in a different manner. Niebuhr says that inner history and inner faith belong inseparably together as the existence of self and an object of devotion for the sake of which the self lives (78). And this relation he now extends to the parallelism which "is something like that of animal faith in the existence of an external world and the data of experience" (79).

> So also the faith of selves in a source of value or in a god is inseparable from the inner experience of selves, from what happens to them in their history. They cannot but believe that these events, the joys and sorrows of the self, have meaning but what the meaning is cannot be known apart from inner history. The necessity of believing in a god is given with the life of selves.... To be a self is to have a god (80).

This is Niebuhr's natural religion. But he does acknowledge that these gods can be "idols . . . products of erroneous imagination." The distinction between these possibilities, Niebuhr says, can only be made "through the experience of inner history" (80).

As part of the "external history of ourselves, communicated to us," which becomes "an event in inner history," through the response we give to it, Niebuhr even mentions Feuerbach and his account of Christianity (85). But as though he had not, he continues to say that

> because the Christian community remembers the revelatory moment in its own history it is required to regard all events . . . as workings of the God who reveals himself (86).

Instead of questioning the reality of the content of this memory he uses it as an instrument for understanding others, even for understanding all the events we may experience. In view of "a particular set of historical experiences" and its use as "the firm conviction of an underlying unity" for the discovering of "the manifestation" of the one "divine self . . . in all other events," he speaks of "an intelligible pattern of reality" (86 f.). He compares this kind of faithful seeing of the outer history to viewing it "with the eyes of God." But this kind of seeing is impossible for man. Yet Niebuhr argues that "what is simultaneous in his case can in a measure be successive for us" (88).

This reasoning of faith Niebuhr describes in his third chapter as "Reasons of the Heart" (91 ff.). First he puts it in contrast to the question "why I am I" which, following Niebuhr, reveals in its obscurities "nothing" (92). In opposition to this he defines revelation as "that part of our inner history which illuminates the rest of it and which itself is intelligible" (93).

At this point he comes for a fourth time to speak of a parallelism between natural science and the faithful interpretation of history. In both spheres, he says, reason uses imagination (95), "concepts, images, patterns . . . symbols" (96). Reason uses anticipated images which have to be proved as apt or inapt. "In our external knowledge reason," he says, "is right imagination" (97). But there are good and evil imaginations. Evil imaginations are made apparent "by their consequences to selves and communities," Niebuhr writes, "just as erroneous concepts and hypotheses in external knowledge are shown to be fallacious by their results" (99). The norm in both cases is their fittingness in the context in which they are used. As pluralistic patterns are bad because they "refuse to be combined into an integrated system," so also are egocentric patterns bad because they lead to alienation and isolation (100 ff.). Under this aspect, for Niebuhr, Christ is the image through which

> deeds and sufferings begin to compose themselves into a total picture of significant action in which the self no longer occupies the center (124).

Christian preaching has to use this "great occasion" not so much as abstract ideas and doctrines, but as a "dramatic image" (126), as "a unique, unrepetitive pattern" (127). In such an interpretation of past, present, and future history, revelation is "subject to progressive validation" (132).

But alongside this validation in history Niebuhr stresses that revelation is not "a tentative hypothesis" that we have freely chosen (139), but it means rather "that something has happened which compels our faith" (139). It has a "self-evidencing quality" (141). While in "objective knowledge the self is the only active being" (144), he says that God, like other persons as selves, makes himself "manifest or he cannot be known" (145) and our activity is the second and not the first. He refers in this context to the idea of Buber that we are known by a 'Thou' and only so do we know ourselves (146). Niebuhr writes:

> We acknowledge revelation by no third person proposition, such as that there is a God, but only in the direct confession of the heart, "Thou art my God" (153 f.).

Corresponding to the prayer which begins "Our Father" one hears in moral law the "Thou art the man" (169). In this way he defines "the revelation of God" as being

> not a possession but an event, which happens over and over again when we remember the illuminating center of our history. What we can possess is the memory of Jesus Christ, but what happens to us through that memory we cannot possess (177).

It is "the beginning of a revolution in our power thinking and our power politics" (187). And for Niebuhr that is basically "the meaning of revelation."

II. AN IMMANENT CRITICISM

Alongside the richness and concreteness of observation and idea in the thought of Richard Niebuhr, I especially acknowledge in it the following points. First, his recognition of what he calls and describes as relativism, the historical conditionedness of all of our knowledge. Second, his idea of patterns in which our knowledge happens; that these patterns are mostly traditional; that they have to be proved adequate by their fruitfulness. Third, the difference between objective, scientific thinking, in which we have to suppress value judgments as much as possible, and personal commitment with respect to things which happen to us and which have to do with the meaning of life. In this latter regard we deal, on the one hand, with our understanding of our fellowmen as thous, and, on the other hand, with the indication therein of the religious dimension—in short, with the indication of a reality which as inner history cannot be proved objectively since it presupposes a confessional standpoint if ever it is to be in some measure intelligibly evaluated in terms of its consequences in the outer world.

In these three points we have a good representation of scientific thinking which endeavors to maintain awareness of its possibilities and limitations and which attempts to be as objective as possible in its methods, respecting the objectivity and historical conditionedness of the standpoint of the observer. Furthermore, when it is said that faith has to do with the question of meaning, that it cannot be generally proved, and that its content is not a possession but takes on reality in personal decision, we have essential elements of what we mean by faith in distinction from scientific knowledge.

Nevertheless, along with our appreciation for this venerable scholar whose thought and personality formed a whole generation of theologians, we must also indicate certain questionable points   73 in his argument and take some positions counter to those set out in his work.

First, we must point to his idea that logic is—like metaphysics, ethics epistemology, and so on—historically relative. That is true only in respect to the historical appearances of systems and uses of logic but not in respect to the basic rules of logic, as expressed in the axioms of identity, the forbidden contradiction, the excluded third, and the relationship of cause and effect within a defined context. These basic rules of logic are not present at every moment of the history of thinking. They can appear and they can be omitted. But they appear with our awakening to thinking-consciousness, and they are inseparable from it. They are a basic structure of our thinking-consciousness and when they are not at hand we do not think but remain only in a kind of dream-thought. They are used even when we pretend that they are not in force, that they are only historical. Only on the basis of their use can they be rejected, but then we are dealing with a thinking which misunderstands itself. They even work in illogical thinking: even the impossible attempt to prove that they are not valid uses them. Logic of this kind is not historical but stands as the presupposition of historical argument. One cannot argue without it.

Second, in the use of logic, methodologically scientific thinking does not proceed only with patterns or images, as Niebuhr says, but with concepts which unequivocally designate their objects. Science proves the aptness or inaptness of its patterns in conceptual thought rather than in more or less vague pictures. It loses in this way the concreteness of the pictorial form of patterns, but only in such abstraction is an unequivocal designation of what we mean possible. Even the interpretation of patterns uses concepts, and actually a pattern itself is a concept. Therefore, it is misleading when Niebuhr uses pattern and concept as synonyms. Concepts are abstractions from patterns but as such they point to the reality which occurs to us in the patterns. Thinking in patterns may be poetry, as Niebuhr asserts, but it is not scientific thinking. Even for the clarification of inner history we need concepts; a justification of experience is only possible with their help. Patterns are more original than concepts, but their scientific evaluation is only possible by conceptual thinking, as Niebuhr's work itself shows. And when Niebuhr does not succeed, the reason lies in his reference to patterns instead of clear concepts.

Third, conceptual thinking is an abstraction from experienced reality, and it proves its results according to appropriate methods carried out in ever new and unending confrontations with the demands of experience in its different realms. But reality as such, the objective existence of things and occurrences, is never a problem for science. It does not ask about reality as such. It knows that it has to do with reality in its conceptual forms but never with reality as such. The scientist is just as convinced that he forms reality through concepts as the historian is in his acknowledgment of the pattern character of history. In this framework both the scientist and the historian are able to know. For the relationship of concepts and even patterns or methods of thinking to their content, they do not need a belief. They do not believe in this reality but they experience in scientific research itself the correctness or falsity of the results of their thinking. But the question whether there is reality at all, if they are solipsists, or the question whether in their concepts being is thinking would be foolishness for them—a hindrance to their thinking. They leave this "boundary" thought to metaphysicians and theologians and other curious people who possess faith in reality. They do not believe in reality because reality in their kind of thinking is not a meaningful problem. They do not know anything about "an unconquerable compulsion" to "belief in reality." It is therefore wrong when Niebuhr says that the scientist has an animal faith in reality and equally wrong when he refers to such an animal faith for the confidence of faith in the reality   **75** of divine actions. This confidence of faith, as Niebuhr describes it, is something else, and that is the *fourth* point at which we disagree with him.

Faith, as Niebuhr understands it, is basically a value judgment. We cannot live without the conviction of meaning for our lives, our world, and history—that is his basic statement and he refers to it as a natural one. In the context of history he is searching for a pattern, for an event which will give the possibility for understanding life as meaningful and for fitting life into a complete view of the world. Such an understanding will then not be deceptive but will have an objective guarantee in the totality of history. Even though this meaningful world can be seen only by faith, it is for Niebuhr not merely a reality of inner history. We do not, as he stresses, have to do with a double reality—and that means that what we mean by faith is valid also for the reality outside of our faith, for the one reality.

If Niebuhr had not said this, he would have held to the standpoint of modern Protestant "faithology" or "religionology" which he has rejected. But what he is doing here is to confuse judgments of value with judgments of being. Out of faith as a value judgment he develops a judgment on the realm of being, the realm of the one reality.

It is significant that at this point he uses the picture of seeing the world with the eyes of God; but he also acknowledges that this is impossible because of the finitude of man. Thus he demonstrates that logic may even be a consequence of a false pretension, that logic is historically conditioned. He does not see that here he is actually confusing a judgment of value with a judgment of being. Such a confusion of two conceptually different standpoints is a possibility for him because of his use of mere patterns instead of unequivocal concepts.

Fifth, to justify this illogical transgression from value-judgments to being-judgments, Niebuhr speaks about the great pattern of Jesus Christ, which in the Christian tradition furnishes us with all that we need for the fulfillment and the guarantee of a meaningful life. Of all the good things which Niebuhr mentions in this context concerning the working of Christ in our minds in respect to guilt and love and our relationships with our fellow men none can destroy the basic fact that we are dealing here with a product of wishful thinking. In this we not only remain in the faithology of post-Schleiermacherian thinking but also fall victim to the Feuerbachian verdict of illusionary thinking. An illusion, to be sure, can also be helpful, but it is nevertheless an illusion when we pretend that we have to do with something other than our faith. Faith becomes notoriously illusionary when we try to assure ourselves of a guarantee for a complete outlook on the world instead of taking upon ourselves the risk of being disavowed by the world. Even the motive of compelling evidence does not help here because nothing else is more compelling for an animal faith than the necessity of securing an objective guarantee for its fulfillment.

At this point I see the greatest weakness in the theology of Richard Niebuhr and the reason for its failure. The weakness and failure are threefold: First, he appeals to a confidence in God's almighty and benevolent governance of the whole world. In this praise of God's good world he is speaking like a representative of the Enlightenment of the eighteenth century or the later Karl Barth. But since he does not share either the rationalistic and optimistic monism of the former nor the latter's supernatural orthodox doctrine of the saving work of Christ, his confidence in the goodness of the world is without a real basis. The only proof he has for his optimistic assumption lies in the confidence in God to which he appeals. But how can he be convinced that God's world is a good one? Not only the realities of the world but also the biblical view of sin and evil and of the fallenness of the creation speak against this presupposition. The only proof he has for it is the fittingness of this confidence as he uses it to interpret the world. He tries to show how this confidence works in our picture of the world and in our practical behavior. But this is more like the attempt of the legendary Münchausen to extricate himself, by pulling on his own pigtail, from the swamp into which he has wandered.

Second, it is easily understandable, in our present understanding of the history of the original Christian hope of the redeeming work of Christ and its expected fulfillment in the eschatological events, that Niebuhr does not refer to this New Testament solution of the problem of theodicy. Nevertheless, Niebuhr's confidence in God is indeed a substitute for the primitive cosmological eschatology which has proved so problematic. In Niebuhr's thought, not only is the biblical eschatological hope of a new creation through the arrival of the Messiah dropped out, but the dualistic world view of New Testament eschatology is also changed into a monistic one. It is hard to see how it could be possible to take into account the eschatological message of Christ in the monistic structure of Niebuhr's view of the activity of God. The distinction between an inner and an outer history is an inadequate substitute for the primitive Christian view of the two aeons, and even this change can be seen as a consequence of the delayed Parousia. But that is not the way to translate the truth of the original view of early Christian eschatology. In comparison to Niebuhr's solution, the traditional Christian acknowledgment of a double revelation—general or natural and special or supernatural—is even more appropriate to the intention of the Christian message of God's special revelation in Christ.

Third, in his struggle for a meaningful interpretation of the biblical message for our day, Niebuhr does not bring to an end the tension between monism and dualism in history. He is right when he tries to transform the mythological world view of the biblical eschatological outlook into an historical one. But his existentialism is too psychological and sociological to interpret sufficiently the existential truth of the crisis which the eschatological message of the New Testament brought about in our self-understanding of world history.

It may, finally, be acknowledged that the greatness of this theologian lies ultimately in his rejection of the idea that any kind of security can be possessed in an objective God or in the history of salvation belonging to such a God. Further, his greatness also lies in his attempt to guide us to a genuine openness toward all other philosophical and religious standpoints, and thus to a renunciation of every kind of theological self-defense. But this openness and renunciation stands in tension with his advocacy of the uniqueness of God's revelation in his Son. The theology of Richard Niebuhr does not provide us with the possibility of witnessing to this uniqueness in such a way that the openness he shows on the other side can be convincing.

It is impossible to do what Niebuhr confesses to be his goal: to combine Troeltsch and Barth.

III. POSITIVE CONSEQUENCES

What are the positive consequences of this encounter with Richard Niebuhr? The following remarks pertain to this and briefly give our estimation.

In the first place, Niebuhr omits from his thinking the real reason why, in all our imaginative and conceptual thoughts, we are not able to possess God and his revelation. The reason is other than the fact that we are always involved in the duality of an objective or outer and a subjective or inner history. This dualism must be taken and understood in a basically different, more all-encompassing manner than Niebuhr employs.

In all our thinking-consciousness we have to do not only with 79 a more or less objective or more or less subjective approach to reality, but with a dichotomy which encompasses every kind of thought, our subjectivity and our objectivity, inner and outer history with all their conceptualities and patterns, and our demand for meaning and its fulfillment as well—even the expressions of our evidence and decisions. This dichotomy is seen in our awareness of the situation in which we find ourselves when we become a thinking-consciousness, our awareness of the fact that we are always a subject directed to objects which are always objectifications for our thinking-consciousness. All that is reality for us is reality in this subject-object schema, and this schema is not a relative one—more or less objective or subjective, outer or inner, uncommitted or committed, personal or impersonal—but an absolute structure of our consciousness. All that we may say or think is involved in this schema.

The subject-object dichotomy is here not a quality of our judgments but a basic structure of our thinking-consciousness. It is at hand as soon as we begin to think and as long as we think. It is not relative but absolute. It can be made into a content of conceptuality. We can think about it, and this we do when we speak about a subjective-objective schema in our thinking-consciousness. But even in doing so, we are within the schema. It is ungraspable; we are not able to encompass it. It encompasses us in our thinking-consciousness. It is intended for this consciousness, and it is all-encompassing. It is our fate. We are confined in it. Niebuhr's allusion to seeing with the eyes of God, a sight not accessible to finite man, can be understood as a mythological expression for this basic situation.

But secondly, since this dichotomy, which is principally different from the duality of inner and outer history encountered in Niebuhr, is ungraspable, so realities also exist that are ungraspable for *this* basic structure of our consciousness, even when they appear within it. There are four such curious realities.

One is the thinking "I," which is, in all its self-objectifications in objectivity and subjectivity, more than can be contained in these objectifications. This is the responsible self, the "I" which is conscious in all its responsivenes of the differing patterns of its responsibility—as Niebuhr shows in his posthumously published book, *The Responsible Self.*[2] But it is significant for his analysis that he uses both terms—responsive and responsible—synonymously. The responsible self is that which makes objectifications and is responsible for them. It is what it becomes through them. It is the nonobjectifiable origin of all objectifications. But as such the responsible self is not objectifiable because it always becomes what it is in the way it understands itself. Its authenticity is enacted only in its responsibility. But what it is in its enactment disappears when we confuse it with its appearances. We would extinguish ourselves if we pretended that in its enactment the responsible self does not exist. In this enactment we have to do with reality in its immediacy even though it is mediated through appearances.

What we thereby assert concerning ourselves we have to concede, secondly, to other persons. That happens when we refuse to treat them merely as an "it" in our subject-object schema, as an objectification, and rather treat them as a "thou," as a person in analogy to our responsible selves. Here much of what Niebuhr mentions in reference to Buber could be accepted, but always in terms of the responsive relations in the nonobjectifiable "I-thou" relationship.

Through our indebtedness to our fellowmen we conquer the false egocentricity in which Niebuhr rightly sees the basic failure of human thinking and behavior, even in religion. The 'thou' is an immediate reality as much as the "I," and it is equally nonobjectifiable. As the "I," so the "thou" too, is more or less objective or subjective only in its appearances, but as the "thou" it is not an objectification in the subject-object schema but takes part in the

[2] H. Richard Niebuhr, *The Responsible Self* (New York: Harper, 1963).

enactment of the "I" as a responsible person in community. The same is to be said about the community of "I and thou." Its personal character goes beyond any objectification and, in practice, beyond any organization and institutionalization. It is the crisis of all such attempts. To *be* in love does not mean to *have* a lover. But love in its reality depends on the kind of knowledge we do have as well as on our thinking about the appearances of the lover and on our relationship to him.

There is, furthermore, a third dimension where we encounter reality with nonobjectifiable immediacies. This is precisely at the point we ask the question which Niebuhr says reveals and leads to nothing, "Why am I and why is there something at all and not nothing?" This question goes beyond all thought which resides in the subject-object schema of our thinking-consciousness, and it does not remain relative in the fashion of our more or less subjective or objective judgments. It transcends this schema in an absolute manner because we are not only not able to survey the whole of being, and we not only do not come to an end in our search for a final cause, but what is reality for us is confined in an absolute manner inside the subject-object schema. And that is not absolute reality. Furthermore, about such absolute reality we are not able to say anything. It is like "nothing" for us—but we cannot say that it is nothing. It could also be reality as such, but it would not be that if we pretended that it is that. We cannot say anything about it, and if we try to do so regardless, then we lose ourselves in contradictions.

When I ask why there is something at all and not nothing, I am confronted with the nothing. But that is not a nonrevelation, as Niebuhr says. For us it can be a kind of revelation: the revelation of the nothing. And this nothing is an immediate reality, the reality of nothingness, the absolute darkness, the abyss.

And now to our fourth point. Even in this abyss which opens itself to the thinking-consciousness, I am this thinking "I," responsible for its enactment and in responsible relation to other egos, to "thous." And when I ask why there are such "thous" in relation to my "I," then I cannot only say that there is nothing. This "I," in its enactment in community with others, is. It is, however, not as an absolute self-creative "I," but as an "I" called to responsibility in community. Here we not only have to do with a nothing, but out of this which is a nothing for thought we hear the call to responsibility. The call is formed in and dependent upon our historical situation; in all its appearances it is historical and relative. Where, however, it becomes decisive for the enactment of our self-understanding in community, it is unconditioned, or we would not meet it at the point of real decision. Here we encounter that reality which is expressed in the mythological language of religion as the one personal God. In encountering this reality, the question of the meaning of life is answered: I am destined to realize my authentic "I" in community with other beings who are themselves destined to this personal community, and the time and space given to us are the realm where this divine destination is to be fulfilled. But we have no guarantee for this fulfillment save the unconditionality with which we realize our intended authentic existence in community—and even this possibility is for faith, because that which we have described here is faith. For faith, there is grace in the continually renewed acknowledgment that in this situation we are granted what the traditional language of theology means by the particular revelation of a special reality—what is called in Christian images the revelation in Christ. This is the proper place to speak about uniqueness as an expression of the character of the unconditionedness realized in an unconditioned decision.

We say this not in view of the exclusive uses of the symbol of Christ as they appear in the patterns of the Christian faith but in view of the content of this symbol, content not bound to a special time of revelation but to all mankind. I hope that it can be said in agreement with Niebuhr that the revelation of this reality is the meaning of revelation and, as such, the reality of faith.   83

Body type, 10 on 13 Times Roman
Display, Times Roman
Paper, G. M. Antique